BRITISH SOCIETY 1870-1970

Studies in Modern Social History

British Society 1870-1970

By

John Salt

Dean of Social Studies, Sheffield Polytechnic

and

B. J. Elliott

Lecturer in Education, University of Stirling

HULTON EDUCATIONAL PUBLICATIONS LTD

©
1975
J. Salt and B. J. Elliott
ISBN 0 7175 0710 6

First published 1975 by Hulton Educational Publications Ltd,
Raans Road, Amersham, Bucks.
Made and printed in Great Britain by The Garden City Press Limited,
Letchworth, Hertfordshire SG6 1JS

Contents

CONTENTS (continued) *Page*

Preface

This book takes certain basic social themes and follows them through the century between 1870–1970. It is hoped in doing this to provide an interesting and useful social history of the last century of British life. Students who wish to discover what was happening in the world outside Britain might refer to a volume on world society by the same publishers.[1] The documentary material for the book *British Society 1870–1970* has been provided by Colin Holmes of the Department of Economic History, the University of Sheffield.

[1] B. J. Elliott with Colin Holmes, *World Society in the Twentieth Century* (Hulton Educational Publications, 1973)

ACKNOWLEDGEMENTS

Acknowledgements are due to the following for their kindness in supplying the photographs used in this book:

Radio Times Hulton Picture Library
The Forestry Commission
The B.B.C.
British Airports Authority
Automobile Association
Wates Limited
Sheffield Corporation

Part I

Britain 1870-1918
by John Salt

Britain in 1870

INTRODUCTION

Social history is about change in the way people live. In modern times, and especially since the Industrial Revolution, such change has come at an ever-quickening rate so that today it is difficult even to keep track of what is happening in our own lifetime. Yet although change may indeed be rapid, mankind's basic needs do not change and it is with these needs and the ways in which they are met that this book is mainly concerned.

Now it is clear that in all ages men and women are faced with the problem of earning a living. What sort of work is available and what sort of wage it will provide will go far to determine what sort of life a family can lead.

In 1870 the majority of jobs for men were to be found in industrial areas. As early as 1851 half the population of Britain lived in urban surroundings and by 1881 the proportion was two-thirds. By 1901 it was to be three-quarters. This was one major result of the Industrial Revolution which had made Britain for a time the richest country in the world. In 1780 the 'average' Englishman had worked on the land: in 1870 he was a manual worker in industry.

In some industries conditions of work had improved as a result of factory acts passed by Parliament earlier in the century. In the cotton industry, which in 1870 employed more than half a million people, factory inspectors helped to enforce acts which prohibited the use of dangerous machinery, prevented the employment of small children and in some cases limited hours of labour. In the mines, where a quarter of a million men laboured in harsh conditions to tear out the coal to feed the furnaces, forges and foundries of a great industrial nation, women and children were no longer employed underground. Yet we must not, on the basis of this evidence, assume that the work of our ancestors had become much lighter. No act of parliament could alter the fact that 28,000,000 tonnes of coal were dug *by hand* in British mines in 1870—indeed even as late as 1900 the percentage of machine-cut coal barely reached one per cent of the total production from our pits.

For the skilled craftsmen, it is true, there was some evidence of an improvement in working life. For some a Saturday half-holiday was becoming a custom by 1870. The wages of groups such as Staffordshire potters and most Sheffield steel craftsmen rose from 1850 onwards. But in 1870, it should be remembered, the unskilled workers in towns outnumbered the skilled. There were also many workers whose working conditions were not protected by factory acts. Among these were the domestic servants, a group more numerous even than the workers in the cotton industry. There were

Coal getting, 1871

also the women who worked in 'sweated' trades such as lace-making and shirt-making, and it is sad but true that even in 1900 there were workers in Woolwich who were paid little more than 2p for every dozen shirts that they made. Nor was child labour a thing of the past: in the years immediately before 1870 it was found that children were being put to work in the hosiery industry at the age of three, and on farms children were paid 4s (20p) a week for such jobs as singling beet. Nor did the fact of going to school keep a child out of a factory: in 1878 there were 31,000 'half-timers' in the woollen industry, that is children who spent part of their day at work and part of their day at school.

In all ages men and women must work. They must also provide houses for themselves and their families, and here in 1870 the story was repeated: there had been some progress, but there were still deficiencies. The days had passed when a northern builder could eke out his mortar by adding street droppings and the waste products of a local ginger beer factory, but the period 1830–70 had seen the building of tens of thousands of 'back-to-back' houses. 'Built in black air', these houses were packed in long rows near the places of work of their occupants. The final destruction of these cramped and gloomy horrors was to take more than a century.

For parents there must be work; for families, houses; for children, it had long been realised, there must be education. Earlier in the nineteenth century schools had been provided by the Churches. At first there had been Sunday Schools, but day schools had appeared later when it was found that money could be saved by employing older and brighter children as 'monitors' to teach the younger and duller ones. From 1833 Parliament had given grants of money to improve the education in these 'voluntary' schools. Inspectors had been appointed to see that the money was well-spent. A system of pupil-teachers had been set up to encourage the apprenticeship of bright boys and girls who wished to become teachers. Finally, a system of 'payment by results' had been created so that in schools which got government aid the teacher's wage depended on how many of his pupils passed the inspectors' tests!

In 1870 the government grant to schools was £415,000. This helped to pay for 11,000 day schools and 2,000 night schools. But, to quote from a famous speech, it was known that 'in Liverpool the number of children between five and thirteen who ought to have received an elementary education is 80,000; but, as far as we can ascertain, *20,000 of them attend no school whatsoever*, while at least another 20,000 attend schools where they get an education not worth having'. Unfortunately the speaker did not explain what he meant by 'an education not worth having', but perhaps he meant the type of school, discovered some years before, where in an attic measuring 10ft (3 m) by 9ft (2·7 m) there had been crammed one master, one cock, three black terriers and forty children!

Apart from work, housing and education, the industrial masses of the new Britain needed protection—protection from violence and theft, protection from disease, protection from filth and, if possible, protection from poverty. These are the major themes of this book.

Now there can be little doubt that, once again, some progress had indeed been made. Sir Robert Peel's police force, established in 1829, had at first worked only in the London Metropolitan area. But other areas had begun to copy its organisation (it was said that in some cases they simply had to, as the more intelligent criminals realised that the Metropolitan area was the place where they were most likely to be caught, a fact which led them to move away from London), and by 1856 every county and borough had to employ a police force which was paid partly out of local rates and partly out of national funds. Even so, the police had a difficult job to do, particularly in areas where there was a good deal of poverty and ignorance. Well might the character in a comic opera sing 'When constabulary duty's to be done . . . the policeman's lot is not a happy one'. In spite of Peel's work the punishment of offenders was still harsh, although even in 1863, five years before the last public execution, an M.P. had complained that 'punishment had become too weak and uncertain to stop crime'!

Mention has been made of the cramped conditions in which the population of Britain's industrial towns lived. In these areas lack of ventilation and sanitation still presented major problems. Rubbish collected in the courts and alleys between houses. Great, foul, stagnant puddles were not unusual, and sometimes entire districts were badly drained. Between 1869 and 1871 an investigation showed that in Liverpool the only way of preventing poor people living in cellars was to fill the cellars with rubble. In Manchester 'the death rate was high, but chiefly among infants'. Yet it is also clear from the reports that some progress had been made. In Newcastle, for instance, the Corporation had built baths and wash-houses and provided hospitals to cope with epidemics. At Croydon £200,000 had been spent on sewers and the death rate cut from 62 to 18 per

Street scene, 1870's

1,000. Still, there was a great amount to be done if people in towns were to be protected from disease: Liverpool had led the way, but in 1870 few towns had Medical Officers of Health.

Yet grim as living conditions could be, life in an insanitary back-to-back house and daily heavy labour were preferable to the fate of those who had no work and had to seek poor relief. In the winter of 1861, for instance, the winter was so cold that work was brought to a stop at the London docks—this was, by the way, one of several very severe winters recorded in Victorian times; in 1837 a bonfire had been lit on the frozen River Don at Sheffield. In 1861, however, more than 1,000 London dockers had to go into work-houses, whilst another 4,000 were set to work breaking stones. Yet another 10,000 families faced conditions which horrified even hard-bitten police magistrates. Once again, however, some progress had been made. At least the development of the country's world-wide markets now prevented the threat of the famines which had been known in earlier centuries. There was also evidence of the development of a more humane outlook: in the 1860's Poor Law Unions had set up dispensaries where the poor could obtain medicine and medical advice; in 1869 the Metropolitan Poor Law Guardians had been given permission to provide training ships for poor boys. But poverty—real, hard, grinding poverty—was still a thing to be feared, and terror of the 'poor house' was a fact of life for many of Britain's population.

Certainly, life in towns in 1870 must seem very hard in comparison with our own age. And, as modern people, we might ask: what made life bearable for ordinary working people in 1870? Partly, one supposes, the lack of knowledge of a more secure, more comfortable existence. It seems to have been accepted, for instance, that toil was the lot of the working man, and phrases that have come down to us—phrases such as 'hard work never killed anyone'—suggest that there was, perhaps a certain pride in all this. For some the chapel provided comfort, whilst others turned to the 50,000 beer houses known to have existed in 1870. Perhaps, too, a writer should mention the companionship which developed in those cramped streets. Families were large (61 per cent of women who married in the ten years after 1870 had five or more children each), and grandparents, aunts and uncles tended to live in the same area as parents and children. For most of these people, indeed, loneliness cannot have been a problem.

Then again, the capacity of human beings to *adapt* to their surroundings cannot be ignored. In particular, children seem to be able to make the best of their world, and many of the games and jingles of childhood were invented in narrow, cobbled streets lit by gaslamps whose light, in 1870, rarely reached 20 candle-power. This, too, was the world of the organ grinder and his monkey, the rag-and-bone man, the one-man band and the 'painless' dentist whose patient's cries were drowned by a roll on his assistant's drums. In many urban areas, too, there was the theatre, the fair, 'the peep show', the boxing booth, and the excited temperance meetings held by societies which were formed to persuade people to avoid 'the demon drink'.

It will have been noted, no doubt, that in describing the life of people in industrial towns in the nineteenth century little has been said about the more prosperous people of the time. One reason for this is very straightforward. In general people who prospered would try to move into surroundings that were more pleasant, often into the suburbs or countryside around the industrial town. As a report in the 1840's had commented, 'those who might advocate a better state of things depart'.

Who were the better-off people? For the time being we shall ignore the country-dwellers and also the very rich, and concentrate on those who could afford to live on the outskirts of towns which had grown up with the Industrial Revolution. Among these were the merchants, newspaper owners, manufacturers, managers and lawyers of the time.

What is perhaps of special importance to note is the huge gap which existed in 1870 between these people and the industrial masses whose life has been described in an earlier part of this chapter. There can be no better illustration of this than a table

A scene from the life of the rich

printed in Mrs. Beeton's famous *Book of Household Management* which explained how many servants could be kept in accordance with the income of the head of a house. The table is, in fact, instructive both because it tells us something of middle class life in 1870 and also because it tells us something about the changing value of money in the last century.

Income	Servants
About £1,000 per year	Cook, housemaid and perhaps manservant.
From £750 to £500 per year	Cook, housemaid.
About £300 per year	General servant.

By twentieth-century standards taxation on income was low. Such were the demands of the middle and upper classes for servants that in 1851 there were one million domestic servants in Britain, one in nine of all women and girls over the age of ten being employed in this way. By 1871 there were about 1,300,000 domestic servants.

When, in fact, we look at the large houses that were built in the Victorian period (and many of these houses, of course, still exist) we can work out, even if we did not know, that they needed large numbers of servants to run them in an age before the vacuum cleaner or even the gas fire was introduced. Simply to keep all the fires burning was a job that required some energy, and the Victorians do not seem to have been afraid to make servants climb endless flights of stairs.

Just as there were very great differences in the lives of the middle and the working classes, so there were very great differences in the education of their children.

By 1851 the middle classes represented some ten per cent of the population, and they showed a keen desire for the education of their children. To a small extent these demands were met by the old-established grammar schools, but in many areas new private day schools were set up—academies, as they were sometimes called—which in a few cases included science in their curricula.

The nineteenth century also saw a great growth of public schools, to which boys were normally sent as boarders. In the social history of the modern age, as we shall see, the importance of the development of transport is likely to be very great, and the first 70 years of the nineteenth century had been no exception to this rule. It was, in fact, the great age of railway building which helped to make possible the movement of more and more children to schools far from their houses. By 1870 the 12 m.p.h. stage coach that had taken

Tom Brown to Rugby was no more: the first *Bradshaw's Railway Timetable* had been published as early as 1839.

Some of the public schools, such as Eton, were already ancient. Others were of more recent origin. There had been considerable improvements in discipline and teaching since the eighteenth century, when soldiers had sometimes to be used to restore order. However, a Commission in 1864 complained that there was still far too much concentration on the teaching of Latin and Greek.

In 1868 another Commission included girls' schools in its report, and here a very gloomy picture was painted. It was rare indeed for a grammar school to admit girls, and even where this happened it was usual for them to leave at fourteen, so that their chances of getting professional qualifications were low. Good quality schools for girls, such as the North London Collegiate School and Cheltenham Ladies' College, were few and far between. Girls were not allowed to sit the examinations of the University of London until 1869, as until then there was no women's college at either Oxford or Cambridge.

Like the poorer people of the towns the middle classes needed protection from violence, theft, disease and economic disaster, although their awareness of these dangers in their most stark forms was perhaps less acute. In 1870 ignorance of 'how the other half lived' was a real factor in British society. The separate education of the children of the two great social classes, and the exclusion of middle-class women from the life of work, were not unimportant reasons why this should be so. Crime was chiefly read about in newspapers—and some papers of the time carried very lurid reports indeed. No doubt the lively imaginations of nannies and servants led to the spread of stories of famous villains like Charles Peace. Diseases such as cholera could strike at rich as well as poor families, and even the children of the well-to-do often died before they reached adulthood. A severe slump in trade could ruin a businessman. But few middle class people could have known at first hand of the horrors of, say, the East End of London in 1863:

'On Saturday night . . . the beer houses are decorated like palaces. Drunkenness is everywhere, but it is joyless, sad and gloomy; a strange silence seems always to prevail. Only now and then do abuse and brutal fights disturb this weary silence which weighs upon you so heavily. The women are in no way behind and get drunk with their husbands while the children crawl and run among them. Many of these husbands thrash their wives dreadfully. The children of these people, almost before they are grown up, go on the streets, mingle with the crowd, and often do not return to their parents.'

We must not assume, however, that the people so described were *typical* English people of the time. Apart from anything else, there were many relatively well-paid and dignified working men in 1870, some of whom were leading supporters of night schools, insurance societies and co-operative organisations. In quoting from the description of the East End of London in 1863 what we are really doing is to point out that ignorance of the lives of the really poor and their problems was widespread at that time.

An age in which ignorance, vice and horror existed in the slums of towns was also an age in which, for some, life seemed to be safer, richer and more rewarding than it had ever been. For the well-to-do this was the age of the large breakfast, the carriage at the door, the dinner party followed by musical entertainment in the home, the crinoline, the garden party, the exciting journey home from boarding school. It was the age when the young were introduced to the delights of *The Water Babies*, the fairy tales of the Brothers Grimm and Hans Christian Andersen: an age which saw the spread of the custom of decorating Christmas trees and the sending of Valentine cards.

But what of life in the country? When the Corn Laws had been repealed in 1846 many people had prophesied that English agriculture would be ruined. Yet this was far from being the case. The years from 1850 to 1870 had, in general, been years of prosperity for British farmers. By 1861 almost all the land in Britain which could be farmed was producing grain or meat.

At various periods in the nineteenth century there were complaints that prospering farmers were spending too much on luxury. Even if such complaints were sometimes false, there must have been some evidence to support them. Thus we are told that the larger farmers, at any rate, often kept no records apart from their bank passbooks: their wives and daughters were 'ladies of leisure': their sons were sent to boarding schools.

For the farm labourers, however, these had been harsh years indeed. As early as 1830 the cruelty with which rural rioters had been treated had shown just how great the gap between social classes in the countryside had become. In 1872 Joseph Arch described farm labourers with 'faces gaunt with hunger and pinched with want'. Not surprisingly, their numbers had fallen by something like one-third from 1851 to 1871. There were many factors to account for their poverty. These included the competition of women and children for men's jobs and the disappearance of the old rural crafts. The picture was not always black, it is true: in the Peak District, for instance, the old custom of the labourer living with the family of his employer had not died out. Similarly, in some areas (and especially the North) wages were up to twice as high as in other areas. Yet in all too many cases low wages went with poor diet and poor living conditions: in 1870 the mud-and-wattle, leaky-roofed cottage was still to be seen in many parts of the country.

Among the landowners were, of course, the very rich, men and women whose great wealth allowed them to live a life apart. Perhaps, indeed, it is the huge gap between the rich and the poor which might be said to be the most distinctive feature of the social life of the nineteenth century.

Here then are the main features of life in 1870. The following chapters consider the development of these aspects of life in the years 1870–1914.

The Industrial Worker

In 1870, as we have seen, the 'average' industrial worker was a male worker in a factory or in heavy industry. To some extent this was still true in 1914, for the industries which had expanded in the first 70 years of the nineteenth century continued to demand more workers. In 1911 there were 620,000 workers in the cotton industry; between 1900 and 1914 some 60 per cent of all merchant ships launched were made in British shipyards; by 1918, it has been estimated, one-twelfth of the population of Britain was dependent on the coal industry.

Yet, in spite of this continued build-up, the nature of British industry and its workers underwent significant change in this period.

In the first place, there was a decline in the number of small, independent workshops in Birmingham, the Black Country and Sheffield. This resulted partly from the greater efficiency of larger firms, partly from the activities of inspectors who reported on unhygienic conditions for which the small workshops were notorious, and partly through the high cost of mechanisation.

Mechanisation was, in fact, the means by which the life of the workers was to be changed, partly for good and partly for bad. In general it could be said that its effects were beneficial when it relieved men of endless, back-breaking toil, but detrimental when it seemed to make pride and skill of little account. At any rate, mechanisation was becoming increasingly common in many industries in Britain. By 1900 industries such as hosiery, footwear, clothing, flour-milling and brewing were almost completely mechanised. By 1913 eight per cent of coal produced in Britain was machine-cut.

It was mechanisation, too, which allowed the development of new industries which were to make the pattern of industrial employment more complex in Britain and again to encourage the appearance of a type of worker who was described as being *semi-skilled*. As a result of the application of science to industry more and more ingenious machines were introduced. To build and to maintain these machines needed skill of a very high order, and the engineering workmen responsible were proud of their craft, but the actual operation of these machines could be left to workers who had a much shorter training.

The best example of all this was, perhaps, the manufacture of bicycles, a branch of light engineering which was encouraged both by the growing popularity of cycling in this period and by the development of a smaller and more efficient steam engine. Originally, bicycles had been built up in small workshops, but gradually the industry became concentrated in a few large firms in Coventry (an old centre of silk ribbon weaving and watch-making) and Birmingham. In these towns standardisation, mechanisation and assembly-line methods allowed the mass-production of bicycles at competitive prices. By 1904 a £6 bicycle was on the market.

The firms making motor cycles and motor cars also appeared in this period, although mass production methods were slower to come than in the cycle industry. Early cars were hand-made, with some parts being imported from abroad. By 1913, however, there were signs of the gradual importation of factory methods. In 1911 the Sunbeam Motor Company was found to have an elaborate jig and tool system with a production line scientifically set out. In 1912 a break-through for British assembly methods came with the appearance at the Motor Show of the Morris-Oxford car produced by W. R. Morris, an Oxford cycle and motor cycle repair shop owner.

Other industries also developed in the period 1870–1914. These included a very important chemical industry and also an

The new engineering

electrical industry. As early as 1901, for instance, there were 47,000 electrical apparatus workers.

All in all, then, as far as the industrial worker was concerned the period 1870–1914 saw changes which, even though they did not profoundly alter the major industries on which the country's wealth had been based, at least led to a greater variety of work and pointed the way to quite revolutionary changes in the twentieth century. It is interesting to note that the Census of 1851 listed 7,000 occupations; the Census of 1881 listed 12,000; the Census of 1901 listed 15,000. These figures point to an increased efficiency in the collecting of information, but they also draw attention to the development of new branches of industry.

In an age when 'basic' industries, such as coal mining, continued to develop, when new industries—such as electrical manufacture—appeared, and when the 'service' industries—such as transport and building—also expanded rapidly, full economic progress was made possible only by a growing labour force. To some extent this was provided by an expanding population generally: to a much smaller extent it was made possible by the increased employment of women workers.

A School of Typewriting, about 1879

Long before 1870, of course, women workers had been employed in textile factories, in a number of specialised manufactures such as matchmaking and in domestic service. Probably there has been a tendency to exaggerate the number of *married* women workers in towns before 1870, but it should be remembered that those who worked in factories would normally be away from home between 6 a.m. and 6 p.m., and it was the desperate need for women to find work in their own houses that all too often encouraged the 'sweated' trades which remained a disgrace until the early years of the twentieth century.

After 1870, however, expansion in a number of fields offered increased opportunities for the employment of women. The growth of office work, coinciding with the introduction of the typewriter, led to a 900 per cent increase in the number of female office workers between 1881 and 1901. The number of women employed in telegraph and telephone services rose from 2,000 in 1881 to 9,000 in 1901. The development of local government (the County Councils Act was passed in 1888) also increased opportunities for employment, as did expansion in the paper, printing, stationery and chemical industries. Moreover, public spending on what today would be called the social services was increasing. The numbers of women employed in teaching rose from 123,000 in 1881 to 172,000 in 1901: the nursing profession expanded from 38,000 in 1881 to 68,000 in 1901.

By 1901 women workers represented 25 per cent of the nation's labour force. In 1903 the *Daily Mirror* appeared, originally as a newspaper for the ordinary British woman.

So far in this chapter attention has been drawn to the type of work which was open to the industrial worker between 1870 and 1914, and in general it could be said that many of the new jobs that appeared did not require the sheer hard labour of some older industries. On the other hand, it would be wrong to assume that the working man entered quickly into better working conditions and increased prosperity.

Better working conditions and increased prosperity came, in fact, only very slowly. In 1871 Michael Bass, M.P. for Derby, produced evidence that 30 or 40 drivers on the Midland Railway had worked average shifts of 19½ hours and in one case a driver had worked as long as 29½ hours. What is amazing is that such complaints persisted into the 1880's and 1890's. Will Thorne, speaking to London gasworks stokers in March 1889 said, 'I know that you have been working 18 hours under hard and difficult circumstances, that many of you must be dead tired; often I have done the 18-hour shift.'

That improvement did come appears to have resulted mainly from three factors: the activities of the trade union movement, the efforts of a number of enlightened employers, and the acceptance by the Government of the need to interfere in industries where conditions were particularly bad.

The development of trade unions was, in fact, one of the major features of British social life in the period 1870 to 1914. The aim of a union was, of course, to protect the worker and, in particular, to safeguard conditions of labour and to maintain wage levels. It gained growing importance if only for the simple fact that as firms got larger it became more and more difficult for the individual worker to deal direct with the management.

For a trade union to be effective, however, four conditions had to be satisfied: adequate numbers, sound finances and organisation, a clear legal position and an established method of working.

Between 1870 and 1914 there was, in fact, a considerable growth in the numbers of trade unionists, although it should be remembered that even in 1900 only one out of every seven occupied males and one out of every thirty-three females in employment were members of trade unions. In 1892 there were 1,233 unions with

1,576,000 members: by 1914 there were 1,260 unions with 4,145,000 members, of whom 437,000 were women. At the same time evidence of a growing talent for organisation was to be seen. In 1912 the National Union of Railwaymen was formed by the amalgamation of a number of separate unions: the new union succeeded in doubling its membership in a mere year and a half. In 1912, too, the trade union movement secured its own newspaper, *The Daily Herald*. In 1914 came the 'Triple Alliance' of the National Union of Railwaymen, the Transport Workers' Federation and the Miners' Federation of Great Britain.

In this process of development the inclusion of trade union members who were *not* highly-skilled craftsmen was of special importance. The 1850's and 1860's had seen a good deal of trade union development (the Trade Union Congress had been formed in 1868 and an Act of Parliament in 1871 had helped to safeguard the funds of the unions against dishonest officials), but the major advances had been in unions of skilled workers such as the Amalgamated Society of Engineers. The latter part of the century, however, saw the appearance of the New Unions.

Unlike the Craft Unions, the New Unions had low subscriptions and offered few benefits except strike pay. Whereas the Amalgamated Society of Engineers, and even the Amalgamated Society of Railway Servants founded in 1871, were in principle 'decidedly opposed to strikes', the unions of the unskilled founded in the 1880's were, in general, highly militant organisations.

An example of all this was the activity of the dockers' organisation. Now, in the 1880's, the life of London dock workers was becoming increasingly desperate. The work undertaken by such men was of a 'casual' nature: a man would not have a regular job but would wait at the dock gate until he was 'taken on' for a particular task which might take only a few hours. What work had hitherto existed had become disrupted by alterations in world trade routes, which were partly the result of the opening of the Suez Canal, and competition between rival dock companies. An able leader appeared, however, in the shape of Ben Tillett, a docker who had the active support of John Burns and Tom Mann, both of whom were members of the Society of Engineers.

Encouraged by the success of the Gas Workers' Union, who had secured a reduction in the length of shifts from twelve hours to eight, the dockers, in August 1889, presented the dock authorities with the following demands:

(*a*) No man to be taken on for a period of less than four hours.

(*b*) Contract and piecework to be abolished.

(*c*) Wages to be raised to 6d (2½p) per hour, with a higher rate for overtime.

At first two unions were involved, but these came together and appointed a committee. The strike itself was characterised by the good order of dockers and aroused a good deal of sympathy. Financial support came from as far away as Australia and allowed a firm stand to be made. Finally the strike was brought to an end on 16th September, Cardinal Manning, the Lord Mayor and Sydney Buxton having played a leading part in getting the two sides together. The bitter struggle for 'the Dockers' Tanner' was at an end, and *The Times* commented on the dockers' 'remarkable victory'. Like the successful strikes of the gas workers and the Bryant and May match girls, the struggle of the dockers illustrated the new willingness of the unskilled to come together and to accept the authority and organisation of the new type of leader that was emerging.

The period 1870 to 1914 was also one which saw a good deal of clarification of the position of trade unions in relation to the law. The 1871 Act, for instance, has been described as 'the principal Act on which the present-day status of Trade Unions is based'. By this Act, trade unions, which were to be registered, were recognised in law. They could sue and be sued, take action against defecting officials, own land and put up buildings. However, they could not use violence or intimidation in the pursuit of their objectives.

Nowadays, one of the main methods of making a strike complete is picketing: that is, persuading fellow employees not to attend for work, normally by standing near the entrance to the firm in question. The Act of 1871 forbade 'molestation', but, as *The Economist* pointed out, 'it is not very easy to say what is molestation and what is not'. Was picketing molestation? If so, the powers of the trade unions would be considerably weakened.

The position was to some extent clarified by the Act of 1875, which allowed *peaceful* picketing.

Another threat to the trade unions came at the beginning of the twentieth century. In 1900 a strike broke out on the Taff Vale Railway, a prosperous concern which had only 124 miles (200 km) of track, but which carried very large quantities of coal from the valleys

Chemical workers

to Cardiff. The cause of the strike was the transfer of a signalman from one district to another against his wishes. At first the strike was unofficial, but subsequently it was recognised by the union, the Amalgamated Society of Railway Servants. There was some violence, and it seems that the General Manager of the railway, one Aummon Beasley, was a 'hard' man who was determined to teach the trade unionists a lesson.

The strike lasted only eleven days, but the Taff Railway Company later sued the Amalgamated Society of Railway Servants and, after losing its case in the High Court, was awarded £23,000 plus costs by the House of Lords as the Court of Final Appeal. The strike, in fact, cost the union some £42,000, and Beasley was awarded £2,000 by a jubilant railway company.

The decision of the House of Lords thus appeared to take away from unions the protection that they thought they had won under the Acts of 1871 and 1875. Significantly, in 1903 a coal strike in Yorkshire led to the Denaby and Cadeby Main Collieries Ltd. suing the Yorkshire Miners' Association for £150,000; in this case the union won the case, but only after a long and worrying fight.

The only remedy for the situation was a new Act of Parliament, something for which the Labour M.P.s who were now beginning to appear at Westminster were keen to press. In 1906, therefore, the Liberal Government secured the passage of the Trade Disputes Act. In future a trade union was not responsible in law for the civil wrongs committed on its behalf. The Act finally established that peaceful picketing was legal and thus greatly strengthened the power of the unions.

Another threat to the unions came a few years later. By this time trade unions were being collected to finance Labour M.P.s who, in turn, gave support to trade unions. As a result of the efforts of the Labour Representation Committee there were 29 Labour M.P.s in the House of Commons, an important asset to the trade union movement. But now the question was: was it *legal* to raise money for this purpose, particularly if there were some trade union members who were unwilling to pay? If the answer was no, then Labour M.P.s who had a special responsibility for protecting the interests of trade unions might find themselves in great difficulties, for in those days M.P.s were still unpaid. This was a serious matter indeed for the unions.

The crisis came when Walter Osborne, a head porter, a trade union branch secretary and a member of the Walthamstow Liberal Association, refused to pay the political levy to the Amalgamated Society of Railway Servants. In 1908 and 1909 the case was fought in the courts, and, as with the Taff Vale Railway dispute, it finally reached the House of Lords. At every stage the political levy was declared illegal.

Once again the union position was saved by an Act of Parliament. The Trade Union Act of 1913 made the political levy legal, provided that the majority of the members of a trade union voted in favour of it. Individual members of a union could 'contract out' (that is, decline to pay the levy) provided they gave notice in writing of their intention to do so. Further, in 1911, an Act of Parliament had provided for the payment of salaries to M.P.s.

Meanwhile there was evidence of increasing expertise in the conduct of negotiations between trade unions and employers. In 1876, for instance, a dispute between the coal owners of Durham and the Durham Miners' Association was settled through the appointment of two arbitrators by each side. The custom of 'collective bargaining' developed: in 1892–3 a strike in the cotton industry involving 50,000 workers and lasting 20 weeks ended when the representatives of both sides met in a country inn and reached an agreement after an all-night sitting. The agreement lasted until 1905. On the employers' side collective bargaining was made easier by the creation of federations: in 1876 a national organisation of building employees was set up and in 1896 it appointed a full-time general secretary. From the industrial workers' point of view the advantage of collective bargaining was that it helped to establish minimum standards in working conditions and wages over wide areas. Some help, it is interesting to note, came from Parliament. The Conciliation Act of 1896, for instance, introduced the Ministry of Labour's conciliation service whereby help and encouragement could be given for the two sides in a dispute to be brought together. By 1910 the working conditions and wages of some $2\frac{1}{2}$ million workers were covered by collective agreements, including arbitration and awards. On the other hand, collective bargaining was slow to develop in some industries, notably the railways where it was considered that the interference of unions in the day-to-day running of the system was inconsistent with public safety.

Lead working—'a killer trade'

In some industries it is possible to trace the direct influence of the unions on the improvement of working conditions. Agitation for some years by the Miners' Federation of Great Britain resulted in the passing in 1908 of the Coal Mines Regulation Act which introduced a statutory eight-hour day, an interesting innovation in that it regulated working hours for *male* workers. In 1912 the Coal Mines Act went further by setting up district boards in 22 coal mining districts and establishing minimum wages.

Where trade unions were weak, or did not exist at all, Parliament felt increasingly obliged to interfere, to improve working conditions. This was particularly true of the 'sweated' industries, such as the making of chains, lace, nails, paper boxes and clothing. The conditions in tailoring, it will be noted, were not helped by the introduction of the sewing machine, which in many cases simply allowed a more furious pace to be kept up. In 1909 the Trades Boards Act struck against long hours and low pay by establishing boards, made up of representatives of employers, workpeople and outside members, which decided wages in what had been notoriously underpaid industries. The wage rates decided were then confirmed by the Board of Trade. Another Act of this period established a weekly half-holiday for shop assistants, an occupation which since 1870 had increasingly been taken over by women.

In general, therefore, it could be said that the nature of industrial work had become more varied between 1870 and 1914, particularly with the extension of light engineering. The employment of females had increased significantly. In general, too, it could be said that overall working conditions had improved, although there were still some disgraceful black spots. It is difficult to prove whether at any given time the average worker was better off in terms of wages than he had been some years before because of the economic depressions which the country periodically suffered. On the other hand, between 1870 and 1914 the *trend* was towards better pay and a higher standard of living. A Wage Index, with 1891 taken as 100, reads as follows:

1871	85
1881	90
1891	100
1901	108

After 1908, it is true, prices rose and wages did not always keep pace, but even so average consumption of products such as tea, sugar and tobacco showed a steady rise in the early twentieth century.

So much for a survey of industrial work. Of equal importance were the conditions in towns where this activity took place. We shall discuss these conditions in the next chapter.

Improvement in Town Life

An important feature of British life between 1870 and 1914 was the continuing growth of British industrial towns. This was partly a result of continued immigration into industrial areas, although this process slowed to some extent after 1880. Essentially, however, it was the product of high population growth which slowed down only after 1911. The average mid-Victorian family contained six children: of every 100 women who married in the years 1870-9, seventeen bore ten or more live children.

What is certain is that if improvements had not come in a number of ways Britain's growing town populations would have produced public health problems of staggering dimensions. It is obvious that no community could long have borne the multiplication of areas such as those described in *The Bitter Cry of Outcast London* published in 1883:

'To get into them you have to penetrate courts reeking with poisonous and malodorous gas arising from accumulations of sewage and refuse scattered in all directions and often flowing beneath your feet. . . . You have to grope your way along dark and filthy passages swarming with vermin. Then, if you are

Slum conditions in 1888

not driven back by the intolerable stench, you may gain admittance. . . .'

The author went on to explain how the average room was 8ft (2·5 m) square, with walls and ceilings literally running with filth. He continued:

'What goes by the name of a window is half of it stuffed with rags or covered by boards . . . you may perchance discover a broken chair, the tottering relics of an old bedstead, or the mere fragment of a table; but more commonly you will find rude substitutions for these things in the shape of rough boards resting upon bricks, an old hamper or box turned upside down, or more frequently still, nothing but rubbish and rags.

Every room in these rotten and reeking tenements houses a family, often two.'

In a limited way such conditions could be dealt with, or at least avoided, by suitable legislation in Parliament. But what is abundantly clear is that Acts of Parliament, in themselves, often achieved very little unless they were backed up by determined *local* action.

Fortunately, the period 1870 to 1914 saw a good deal of development in the field of local government. Indeed, many of the great public buildings in our towns, such as the town halls and libraries, date from this period. Blackened by the smoke of years, they are now being cleaned and restored to something like their original appearance. The Local Government Act of 1871 created a Local Government Board under a Minister. This Board was responsible both for the Poor Law and Public Health. Poor Law Inspectors became General Inspectors, with responsibility for oversight of public health arrangements.

In 1872 the whole country was divided into sanitary districts, and each district was required to have a Medical Officer of Health and an Inspector of Nuisances.

Three years afterwards came the monumental Cross Act, of which it has been said that 'it contained a sanitary code more minute and elaborate than any that has been adopted by a civilised country'. The Act of 1875, in fact, brought together all the regulations made during the previous 30 years. If clarified the responsibilities of the sanitary districts, the powers of which were extended to home drainage, water supply, offensive trades, food inspection, infectious diseases and lodging houses.

In 1888 the organisation of local government was strengthened by the creation of County Councils, including the London County Council. In 1900 twelve metropolitan boroughs were created for London and these remained the principal units of local government with the greater area until 1965.

Modern local government has, of course, an incredible range of responsibilities, but to many of those people who were concerned with the quality of town life the issue of housing was of paramount importance. As one reformer sadly commented, 'the housing ruins all'.

To look into the question of town housing in the last quarter of the nineteenth century is to lift the lid off a whole complex of problems. In the first place, of course, the towns themselves had inherited from an early age a huge amount of thoroughly bad housing. A good deal of this housing was owned by relatively poor people who could not afford to improve it or, in many cases, even to keep it in repair. The problem was complicated by the fact that so-called 'offensive trades' (including haddock-smoking!) were often carried on in ordinary dwelling houses. Part of the problem, too, derived from the original cramming together of houses, with up to 40 units being built to the acre (0·4 hectares). But even if local authorities had had the enthusiasm and the powers to knock down slums and rebuild houses, they would have been chary of moving workers too far from their places of employment in an age where there was very little in the way of public transport.

It is also questionable whether many families could have afforded higher rents for better accommodation or whether indeed such accommodation could have been built, for house-building tended to fall off in the bad years, such as 1875–7, when trade was slack.

Various governments made attempts to approach this problem of housing. The Artisans' Dwelling Act of 1875 gave local authorities powers to pull down the worst slums and to replace them out of public money. Joseph Chamberlain, the go-ahead Mayor of Birmingham between 1873 and 1876, was chiefly responsible for the institution of a programme of slum clearance under this Act, but little was done elsewhere. The report of a Royal Commission on Housing which sat in the years 1884–5 was, in fact, a very gloomy one, with attention being drawn to faulty drains, poor water supply, imperfect foundations, inferior building materials, inadequate lavatory accommodation, dampness, filth and vermin. The main conclusion was a painful one: 'Existing laws were not put into force, some of them having remained a dead letter from the date when they first found place in the statute book.'

It is impossible, therefore, to point to a general improvement in housing standards deriving from a single Act of Parliament in this period. It was not until 1919 that a housing act of major importance was passed. Yet improvement undoubtedly came between 1870 and 1914. Partly this was due to groups of reformers in particular towns. The enthusiasm and drive of these groups allowed them, in spite of all difficulties, to set the pace in improvement. Liverpool thus took the lead in the 1860's, Birmingham in the 1870's, London, which took advantage of the Housing of the Working Classes Act of 1890, in the ten years before 1900. In these towns, and in others which copied them, housing gradually improved as local by-laws regulated the heights of ceilings, the size of rooms and the provision of sanitation.

The building of back-to-back houses in Birmingham ceased about 1870, and other towns came gradually to follow this example. In Glasgow and elsewhere slum areas were knocked down simply because traffic congestion required that main streets be widened. By 1912 new building in some areas of Britain had cut the death rate of their populations by 50 per cent, although even in 1913 only one house in ten in Middlesbrough had proper drainage.

Gradually the number of houses in Britain increased, although it must be remembered that many of the older houses needed really to be replaced at a rate of 60,000 per year at least.

Year	Houses
1871	4,520,000
1891	5,824,000
1901	6,710,000
1911	7,550,000

A falling-off in the rate of production after 1903 was to some extent compensated for by a fall in the birthrate. In 1914, however, there was still a housing shortage and this was to remain a problem in British life in the twentieth century.

London scene, 1904

Improvement in the standards of British housing thus came partly from the determination of enthusiasts to improve their towns. It also derived from the development of transport facilities which in time allowed for the appearance of suburbs. The problems of travelling from home to work were gradually being overcome. This was particularly true of London.

In London horse-drawn trams became numerous in the 1870's. Electric versions of these vehicles were tried out between 1889 and 1893 and ultimately became a great success. In 1899 the first petrol-driven bus, a German-built Daimler, appeared in the metropolis, and by 1907 such vehicles had largely superseded the older horse-drawn variety which dated from about 1850.

Even before the age of the electric tram and the motor bus, however, the incredible congestion of London streets had encouraged the idea of underground railways. This was an idea that had aroused some considerable opposition when it was first suggested by Charles Pearson. The proposed tube line was attacked as a 'sewer railway': it was suggested that its construction and operation would weaken existing buildings and that, in any case, it was wicked to tunnel under the feet of decent citizens! The North Metropolitan Railway was formed in 1853, but it was not until 1863 that the Paddington to Farringdon Street line was opened after bitter opposition. Known as 'the Drain', this line was notorious for its smoke and smell. Electrification was to come, however: in 1900 an electrified 'tuppenny tube' was opened by the Prince of Wales, and by 1905 the basis of an electrified underground system had been laid.

The first taxi cabs to arrive on the London streets in 1903 were not very successful, but cabs made by the French firm of Renault were introduced in 1906. One of their advantages was that they had a taxi meter which showed the fare. The London taxi had come to stay.

Also important were the suburban railways, with special train services and special fares. It was these railways, along with the tramways, which allowed London's growing population to be distributed among the suburbs of what was to become the Greater London area. At first it was the middle classes who tended to move to the 'railway suburbs', and indeed many of the imposing villas that were built for them after 1870 are still to be seen, often near to the original stations. Subsequently with the development of the bicycle and also the Cheap Trains Act, working men and women also tended to move from the inner areas of the city.

With the development of railways, then, an increasing number of people working in London became 'commuters', travelling into the city daily. The effect of this was startling. Between 1867 and 1901 the population of London doubled, but the population of Greater London increased by ten times. The actual City shrank, many of its houses being demolished to make way for commercial buildings. In 1801 the population of the City was 120,000. By 1901 it was a mere 26,000. Meanwhile the population of West Ham rose from 2,500 in 1801 to 267,000 in 1901. Hammersmith, another suburb, grew from just over 2,000 in 1850 to 150,000 at the beginning of the twentieth century.

One consequence was, of course, that the countryside was eaten away. A reminder that the Bexleyheath area of London, now a well-populated suburb, was originally an apple-growing area is afforded by the inclusion of apples on the badge of the borough. Perhaps, in the conditions of the nineteenth century, this loss of agricultural land was not too high a price to pay: the alternative was the crowding of people into town and city centres where life must have become increasingly intolerable. On the other hand, one feels that many chances for building really pleasant suburbs were lost. The 'speculative builder' was faced with the challenge of putting up a great number of houses quickly and cheaply. In many cases this was done by building standard houses in long rows. Often building standards were not high, and sometimes the land itself was badly chosen.

What was true of London was also to some extent true of other large towns. Birmingham developed its railway suburbs of Selly Oak, King's Norton and Handsworth. Tramways everywhere also helped to push out the suburbs: westwards of the centre of Sheffield small stone buildings still mark the successive termini used as the tram services ultimately extended almost to the edge of the moorland. Between 1881 and 1901 the numbers employed in the tramway services rose from 2,600 to 18,000. Liverpool had gone over to electric tramways in 1898, and by 1909 there were 2,300 miles (3,700 km) of electric tramway in Britain.

Improvement in building and in many cases the dispersal of town populations made possible by advances in transport thus did something to improve the quality of life in British towns after 1870. So did a general improvement in the provision of amenities, although here again it is possible to point to a very patchy development indeed.

The figures speak for themselves. In 1898 some £1,100,000 was spent on refuse disposal: by 1908 the sum had risen to £2,100,000. In 1883 only £600,000 was spent on sewerage; by 1900 it was £1,800,000 and by 1908 it had reached £4,600,000. In 1884 £900,000 was spent on public lighting: by 1902 it was £1,900,000 and by 1908 £2,200,000.

Increasingly, but with occasional black spots, British towns were becoming better cleaned, better drained and better lit at a time when, as we shall see, advances were being made in education and public health. Moreover, it was considered necessary, at least in some towns, to have parks and open spaces.

As in so many other aspects of national life, science was playing its part. The perfection of the turbine now allowed for the generating of electricity on a large scale. As early as the 1870's there had been experiments in the lighting of town streets by electricity, but the invention of the incandescent burner gave gas an advantage in the 1880's. At first gas was, in fact, a very tough competitor as gas mantles for lighting and gas appliances for cooking and heating were evolved.

By 1900, however, gas and oil for lighting were giving way to electricity. In 1896 Islington became the third London district to have its streets illuminated by electricity. At Deptford a huge power station, designed by Sebastian de Ferranti whilst still in his twenties, was capable of supplying 33,000 lamps. In 1903 some three million tons of coal per year were used to generate electricity: by 1913 this had risen to 4·9 million tons.

In this chapter we have concentrated on the physical conditions in which people lived. It should be remembered, however, that what is often termed the 'quality of life' is equally important. We shall take up this theme in the next chapter.

The Progress of Education

In 1870 the education of the nation's children was in the hands of 'voluntary' schools run by the Churches. In some cases these were quite good schools by the standards of the time, but even where good schools existed it was often impossible to provide sufficient places. In some areas only one child in five went to school and for some children their life at school lasted less than a year.

Yet, as industry developed, there was a growing need for educated people. It is difficult to give technical training to individuals whose minds have not been trained in other ways. Britain was still the 'workshop of the world', but the fear grew that if she did not educate her people she would be left behind by other nations: in 1867 the Paris Exhibition indeed tended to show that the superiority of English goods was not as marked as it had been at the Great Exhibition of 1851 in London. In 1867 the working man in towns had been given the vote, and there was a growing fear that ignorant men might use their votes unwisely. Then again, it had long been recognised that ignorance and crime often went together.

These were powerful arguments, and influential 'pressure groups' sprang into existence to use them. Among these was the National Education League, founded in Birmingham in 1869, which called for free education for all children. To get an Act of Parliament passed setting up state schools was no easy matter, however. Apart from the cost of the schools (and people in those days were very unhappy about the state spending large sums of money), there was a widespread belief that in a free country parents ought not to be forced to send their children to school. Employers of child labour, particularly farmers, were against state education.

Moreover, there were still those who argued that a good workman did not need education. Britain, it was pointed out, was richer than other countries with educational systems: as late as 1899 Charles Booth, comparing it with other countries, could refer to Britain as 'this land of abounding wealth'.

Perhaps, however, the most important obstacle to the development of state education was the opposition of religious groups. Both the Church of England supporters and the Nonconformists tended to be suspicious of the introduction of state education. This attitude derived partly from a suspicion of what was often termed 'Godless' education, a hangover perhaps from the days when it had been asserted on more than one occasion that to teach a man to write without at the same time teaching him to think about religion was to encourage forgery. Each of the two religious organisations was also afraid that its rival might secure some advantage if the state were to interfere in education in a more thorough-going way.

An attempt to solve these problems was made by the Education Act of 1870. The Act was introduced to Parliament by W. E. Forster, the Quaker Vice-President of the Education Department, who was the son-in-law of the famous Dr. Arnold, Headmaster of Rugby School. In many ways it was a very cautious piece of legislation. As Forster himself said, 'Our object is to complete the present voluntary system, to fill up gaps . . . not to destroy the existing system in introducing a new one.'

Where existing schools were found to be inadequate, School Boards were to be elected by rate payers. These Boards were to have powers to raise a local rate, to build schools and to employ teachers.

In the new Board Schools there was to be religious teaching, but it was not to represent the ideas of any particular church or sect in the Christian faith. Teachers in Board Schools could choose not to take part in this aspect of school life, and parents were to be allowed to withdraw their children from religious instruction lessons. For this reason Scripture lessons were held at fixed times, usually at the beginning of the school day.

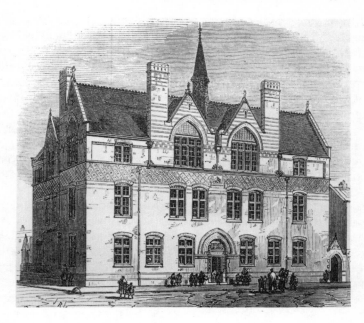

A London Board School in 1874

The Act, then, did not sweep away the Voluntary Schools. These could retain financial support from the Government, subject to certain provisions. Even by 1895 there were only 1,900,000 children attending Board Schools, whilst a further 2,400,000 attended Voluntary Schools.

Further evidence of the cautiousness of the Act of 1870 was provided by the *discretionary* nature of some of its clauses. In particular it will be noted that it was left for each School Board itself to decide whether education should be made compulsory for the children in its area. The Act did not make education free, but a local School Board, could, if it so wished, remit fees in cases of extreme family poverty.

In some ways, therefore, the Education Act of 1870 appears to have been something of a ramshackle measure, although a leading journalist of the day commented, 'I think that Mr. Forster has hit on the only plan that will work in so curious a country as England'. Then again, the Act provided a basis for future advance.

In 1876 Parliament decided that where a School Board did not exist there should be a School Attendance Committee which could introduce by-laws to enforce attendance. Employers were to be fined if they employed children under the age of ten, or children between the ages of ten and thirteen who did not possess certificates to show that they had mastered the three Rs. This, however, raised the problem of the dull child, and thus a curious device, known as the Dunce's Pass, was introduced, the certificate attesting that the child had at least *attended*!

In 1880 the Mundella Act moved away from discretionary legislation by compelling every School Board and Attendance Committee to make by-laws enforcing attendance at school up to the age of ten.

This in turn raised the problem of school fees. It will be recalled that the 1870 Act did not provide free education, although it allowed School Boards to remit fees for the very poor. In 1887 thirteen per cent of all the children on the registers of London Board Schools had their fees remitted. Yet not all areas were as generous as this, and it was obviously unjust both to prevent a poor child from going to school and then to take his father to court.

In 1891 Lord Salisbury introduced 'assisted education' whereby a grant of 10s (50p) per child could be made to schools which applied for it: at the same time parents were given the right to ask for free places for their children. Within four years some four million children were going to school free of charge, although school fees for elementary education were not abolished until 1918.

Although Parliament helped by passing the Acts described above, the real problem of ensuring that the nation's children were educated fell to the men and women who worked locally. There were, in fact, numerous problems to be wrestled with. In some areas it was difficult to find suitable people to sit on the School Boards: in other areas the Boards themselves were too small to support viable schools. Everywhere, as the population expanded, it became a race against time to provide sufficient places. In London an additional 8,000 places were needed every year. Between 1872 and 1880 the London School Board built 197 schools, but even so, and particularly in the early stages, accommodation was so short that children had to be taught under railway arches.

Poor attendance was an additional problem. In 1882, for instance, one in six of the population had names on school registers, but only one in nine attended regularly. Difficult problems sometimes require harsh measures and the Sheffield School Board established what was really a truants' prison in the Rivelin Valley. In spite of the efforts of 'school-bobbies', who checked on non-attendance, there were always some children who never went to school at all.

In spite of Sherlock Holmes' flattering description of Board Schools as lighthouses with beams bravely piercing the dark of ignorance, the schools themselves were often grim places. To some extent London set the pattern in architecture, with its ugly, three-storeyed buildings of great solidity and durability. Matters might have been better if the system of 'payment by results' had not persisted for some 30 years after 1870. Rote learning (e.g. of all the major towns of France) was the order of the day, and this led to the neglect of the bright and the bullying of the dull. Faced with teaching a class of 100 or more, the teacher all too often fell back on the use of the cane to keep order and stimulate effort. The punishment books of the period tell their own story:

'Fred Dewkes—for throwing snowballs at the school clock—2h 4p.' (*i.e. two strokes on the hand and four on the posterior!*)

This was the system which 'drove the teacher and the teacher must drive the child'. Teaching, it was later complained, became 'din-din-dinning'. The harsh teacher became a tyrant, the weak became, at least in the slums, the target for abuse and violence.

Yet gradually problems were overcome and progress made. By 1886 there were 5,000,000 school places for a total population of 28,000,000. By 1895 there were 5,235,887 children at school, some four million of whom were under the age of ten. By the same year, too, 97 per cent of all males were able to sign marriage registers. By 1899 the school leaving age was raised to twelve.

Gradually, too, school became more interesting as new subjects were introduced. After 1876, for instance, subjects such as history and geography were brought in. In the higher standards sciences, and even French, began to appear. After 1896 schools were encouraged to experiment with new methods of teaching reading and arithmetic. Singing and physical education were added to the curriculum, and schools began to organise visits to museums and other places of interest.

For the bright in the Elementary School, however, there still remained a good deal of frustration and blocked opportunity. The 1870 Act did not provide for the establishment of special schools or even classes for the older, intelligent individual who wanted to 'get on in life'. In 1888 a witness told a Royal Commission that 'it would be next to expecting a boy out of the London Board Schools to take wings as to expect him to advance by his own efforts to the University'. A few School Boards did try to find ways to overcome this problem, but their efforts were discouraged. Few boroughs attempted to provide opportunities under the Technical Instruction Acts of 1889–91.

In 1895 the Bryce Commission reported on this state of affairs. It attacked 'the iron machinery of payment by results', condemned the lack of opportunity for bright children in elementary schools and recommended a re-planning of the administration of English education.

In 1902 the Balfour Education Act abolished over 2,500 School Boards and 800 Attendance Committees and replaced them by 300 County and Borough Councils, each with its Education Committee. What had been 'Board Schools' now became Council Schools. Voluntary schools continued to exist, but were now supported from municipal rates as 'non-provided' schools—something which greatly angered Nonconformists in some areas, who for a lengthy period refused to pay their rates to support Church of England schools.

By the terms of the Balfour Act, Local Authorities were given powers to set up Secondary Schools. A further Act of 1907 required all Secondary Schools aided by Local Authorities to give a quarter of all places to pupils winning places from Elementary Schools. Some areas, therefore, at first chose to support what had been private schools, whereas others almost from the beginning provided their own secondary schools. For the children of the fairly prosperous, school fees were thus kept at reasonable levels: for the intelligent children of poor families a 'ladder' was now provided for them to secure education and employment more suited to their natural talents.

Once again, the statistics tell their own story. Note the rise in public expenditure on education:

1870	2·8 million
1884	4·5 million
1900	8·8 million
1914	30·6 million

In general this represented startlingly good value for money, for by 1914 not only had an educational system been created, but some advances had been made in technical education after the Act of 1889 allowed rate support. Scientific education was encouraged by the building of laboratories at the universities of Oxford and Cambridge in the second half of the nineteenth century and also by the creation in 1906 of the Imperial College of Science and Technology in the University of London. Moreover, the last years of the nineteenth and the early years of the twentieth centuries saw the appearance of provincial ('red brick') universities in such towns as Manchester, Birmingham, Leeds and Sheffield.

Meanwhile, there had been continued modernisation in the ideas and organisation of the public schools encouraged by the Public Schools Act of 1868 and the Endowed Schools Act of 1869. The curricula were progressively widened, and some public-school endowments were extended to assist the education of girls.

Law and Order

In 1897 a newspaper warned those of its readers who intended to join the crowds joining Queen Victoria's Jubilee celebrations to 'take off your presentation watch and chain. It never did keep time, and pickpockets must live.' Petty thieving was, in fact, very common in British society at the beginning of the twentieth century, but in many areas there was evidence of a fall in crimes of violence in the second half of the nineteenth century and also of a more general respect for the forces of law and order. In the 1870's assaults on policemen totalled some 13,000 per year; by the 1890's the number had fallen to 11,000; in the first few decades of the twentieth century it was to be reduced to 6,000.

There were many reasons for these changes in attitudes and habits. The general rise in the country's prosperity may well have been some significance, although people in the nineteenth century were slow to appreciate the possible link between poverty and crime. The attack on drunkenness which began with the Licensing Act of 1872 was clearly a factor in the situation. The general improvement in town life, the extension of leisure facilities and the spread of elementary education after 1870 can also be mentioned. This chapter, however, is mainly concerned with changes in the police forces, the courts and the nation's prisons.

In the earlier part of the nineteenth century, Sir Robert Peel had worked on the principle that a more certain detection of crime was a greater deterrent than harsh and inhuman punishments. This had been the reasoning behind the creation of the Metropolitan Police in 1829, and to some extent it underlay the subsequent development of police forces later in the nineteenth century.

The London area, with its huge and growing population, did, of course, present special problems, and this stimulated a number of pioneering ventures by the Metropolitan Police Force. In 1878, for instance, the Criminal Investigation Department was put on a proper basis (detectives had existed before, but unfortunately had been confused in the popular imagination with spies), and in 1890 all departments were brought together at 'the Yard', police headquarters built on land which had originally been intended as the site of an opera house. In 1901 the Metropolitan Police began to collect finger prints, and in 1907 women were attached to the C.I.D. for taking statements from and looking after girl victims of certain types of crime. There were to be no women constables, however, until the 1920's.

In general, other forces tended to follow the Metropolitan lead, but sometimes innovations came from the provinces. In 1909 the systematic classification of offenders according to their criminal

Problems for the police

habits began in the West Riding. The extension of telegraphic and telephone services also increased the efficiency of police forces, as did the introduction of the bicycle.

Between 1880 and 1913 local authority expenditure on the police rose from £3·1 million to £7·5 million. At the same time grants from the Government, which in the case of each authority depended on the securing of a satisfactory report from one of Her Majesty's Inspectors of Constabulary, rose considerably. The total number of policemen rose from about 32,000 in 1881 to 45,000 in 1901: in 1881 there was one policeman to every 799 of the population, but by 1901 there was one policeman to every 724.

Ultimately, of course, much of the success of a police force depends on its capacity to win the support and respect of the public, and here, too, there was evidence of progress. As police pay and conditions improved, the questionable practice of tipping constables slowly died out. There were no national rates of pay established in this period, but in general it was true that whilst in 1870 a policeman's pay had been roughly equivalent to that of a farm labourer, by 1900 it compared favourably with the wage of a skilled craftsman. Moreover, the Police Act of 1890, which consolidated earlier acts, also made provision for police pensions.

Such improvements were wholly justifiable, not only in that they increased the self-respect of the man on the beat, but also in that police work itself was becoming more complicated as regulations for the protection of society multiplied. In the 1860's the training of a constable had been almost entirely limited to foot drill, but in the 1890's a recruit was given training in law and basic duties and attached for a period to an experienced police officer before being given a beat of up to 20 miles (32 km) to patrol.

Whilst the police force was being strengthened and improved in efficiency some important changes were taking place in the administration of the law and the organisation of the prison system.

By 1870 most of the great prison buildings of this country were already in existence. The custom, as is well known, had been to build great blocks of cells radiating from a central point. Such architecture was, in the future, to limit prison reform, but even so a number of very significant developments took place between 1870 and 1914.

In 1878, three years after the disappearance of the last prison hulk of the type described in Charles Dickens' *Great Expectations*, all local prisons were brought over to state ownership. Henceforth they were to be administered by the Government through the Prison Commission. The way was now paved for a more general reform.

In this reform the foundations had been laid by Sir Walter Crofton, the pioneer of the 'Irish System' of prison administration which allowed a prisoner to move progressively from solitary confinement to work on a project with other prisoners to a more 'open' situation in which a considerable degree of freedom and responsibility was allowed. These ideas influenced British prisons generally. By 1914 there had been considerable progress in the provision of prison workshops. A system of remission as part of a sentence for good conduct had also been introduced.

Perhaps, however, the most important step was taken in respect of the treatment of young offenders. Already, in the nineteenth century, progress had been made in the segregation of different *types* of offender—e.g. hardened criminals from first offenders. The Broadmoor Institution for the criminally insane had also been opened in 1877. In 1902 Sir Evelyn Russell-Brise was responsible for the opening of the first Borstal, so-called because it was opened at Borstal, near Rothermere in Kent. Made possible by the Prevention of Crime Act, the Borstal was designed to give education and industrial training to offenders between the ages of 16 and 21. This was a feature of the British penal system which was to be observed and widely copied abroad.

The period 1870 to 1914 also saw some attempts to make the administration of the law more efficient and fair. In 1869 imprisonment for debt, which had earlier consigned many unfortunates to the horrors of the Fleet Prison, was abolished except in cases where the judge was satisfied that the debtor had not wilfully defaulted. In 1879 the prosecution of offenders became more systematic with the appointment of a Director of Public Prosecutions. The Criminal Evidence Act of 1898 allowed the accused to give evidence on his own behalf. In 1907 the Court of Criminal Appeal was instituted, following the tragic case of Adolf Beck, an innocent man who had a 'double' with criminal habits.

Meanwhile, steps had been taken towards the establishment of a system of probation. Acts of Parliament in 1877 and 1879 allowed magistrates to suspend sentences upon first offenders under probation. The Police Courts Mission was established in 1876 by the Church of England Temperance Society and this proved to be the forerunner of a system of probation officers. The Probation of Offenders Act came in 1907 and a few years afterwards came the

National Association of Probation Officers, although probation was not widely used by the courts until after the First World War.

Similar progress was reflected in the treatment of child offenders. Up to 1908 children were tried in public in the same way as adults in ordinary courts. The Children's Act of that year, however, apart from gathering together a large number of earlier regulations relating to children, established Juvenile Courts.

The Nation's Health

Although the improvement in the state of the nation's health between 1870 and 1914 appears modest when compared with progress in the later twentieth century, statistical evidence points to at least *some* general improvement in the earlier period. For instance, the total death rate per thousand fell from 21 in the 1870's to 14 by the late 1890's. The life expectation of the average male rose from 46 years in 1902 to 52 years in 1912. The number of deaths from tuberculosis in England and Wales fell from 61,000 in 1900 to 51,000 in 1910.

There were, of course, many reasons for this important development in the life of the nation, and various of these have been touched on in other sections of this book. Improvement in working conditions was obviously important; a general rise in the standard of living, particularly between 1860 and 1890, seems to have played its part, as did a rise in the standard of education.

In the latter part of the nineteenth century, however, it is possible to see evidence of changes in personal habits. Whereas earlier in the nineteenth century the average person used 3·6 lbs (1·5 kg) of soap per year, by 1891 the figure was 15·4 lbs (7 kg). Between 1881 and 1911 the number of workers employed in laundries rose from 3,000 to 13,000. If Britain was becoming a cleaner nation, she was also becoming a less drunken one. The peak of beer consumption per person was reached in 1899. From 1872 onwards a series of licensing acts limited the number of public houses and restricted their hours of opening.

There were other highly important changes in the nation's diet. It is true that the scientific understanding of nutrition came late in this period: it was not until 1911 that a Polish chemist succeeded in isolating and identifying vitamin B. But, in general, wives and mothers seem to have taken the opportunity of rising wages and an increasing and varied supply of food to improve the average family diet.

In the 1870's the introduction of the steam trawler made possible the increasing consumption of fresh fish. The development of market gardening was also important. Tomatoes, for instance, were cultivated in large quantities from the 1890's onwards, and the expanding sales of fruit with a high vitamin C content further enriched the nation's diet. From 1880 onwards the national switch to pasture farming augmented the home supply of milk, butter and cheese at a time when imports of the two latter commodities were coming from Denmark and other Baltic countries.

The development of refrigeration also helped. In 1880 the first frozen lamb from Australia appeared in London markets.

All this resulted in a general change in Britain's diet, with a swing away from the eating of huge quantities of bread, and an increased consumption of meat, cheese and other dairy products. In 1891 Charles Booth reported that in the case of working class people with small regular wages 'bacon, eggs and fish appeared regularly in the budgets. A piece of meat cooked on Sunday served also for dinner on Monday and Tuesday, and puddings, rarely seen in Class B ("the very poor") were a regular institution, not every day, but sometimes in the week.' In 1899 it was said by another commentator that 'the sort of man who had bread and cheese for his dinner forty years ago now demands a chop'.

If food was becoming more plentiful and more varied, it was also likely to be purer and more hygienic. This arose partly from the action of Parliament. For instance, the Food and Drugs Act of 1875 required Quarter Sessions to submit to the Home Secretary reports prepared by the public analyst on the condition of food. A campaign was, in fact, waged not only against impure food, but also against food that had been deliberately adulterated—e.g. flour mixed with chalk. The Sale of Food and Drugs Act of 1899 was important here, although, once again, a good deal depended on the vigilance of local inspectors.

The cause of hygiene was helped by advances in the more scientific production of food. The manufacture of tinned food was, for instance, encouraged by the introduction of the pressure cooker in 1874. Large-scale biscuit manufacture, which began when J. D. Carr, a baker of Carlisle, converted a printing machine into an automatic cutter, also developed. The application of factory methods to chocolate-making allowed Rowntrees of York to produce 400 brands by 1890.

Other factors of importance were the development of 'chains' of larger stores who were keen to advertise the purity and good quality of their wares. These included the Co-operatives, and also the Lipton, Maypole and Meadow Dairy shops. The first Lipton shop was opened in 1871 and the Meadow Dairy was established in 1901 by Mr. Beale, a former manager with Maypole. The multiple shops, often in working-class districts of large cities, did much to raise general standards, although their impact on working-class eating habits was not always as sharp as might have been expected: before 1914 less than 2 per cent of British food expenditure was on margarine.

Another famous store chain was started by Jesse Boot, a self-made man who had begun work at the age of 13, three years after the death of his father. The Boots Pure Drug Company was first registered in 1888 and by 1896 it had 60 shops in 28 towns. The project had been launched with the use of a new device: the telegram. Two hundred were sent out with the message 'Visit Our Exceptional Display of Sponges at Goose Gate'.

In spite of all this progress, however, it is possible to point to a number of notorious black spots. It has been observed, for instance, that whereas the cattle plague of 1866 was no bad thing in the long run in that it helped wipe out many of the insanitary 'town dairies' of London, Britain was slow to stamp out animal and crop diseases on her farms. An even more serious problem was the health of the very young. Between 1850 and 1900 there was no real improvement in infant mortality rates, and even after that date rickets—that is, bone deformation resulting from vitamin D deficiency—remained all too common. The increased availability of artificial foods for small babies in the early twentieth century was not always a good thing. Such foods were often associated with vitamin C deficiency which caused scurvy.

In 1899, however, the first Infant Welfare Centre was opened in St. Helens. This was concerned with the giving of advice to poor mothers and the distribution of free milk. By 1906 there were more than twelve such centres. Meanwhile, Manchester had pioneered the development of a system of health visitors.

The health of school children also occasioned some alarm, particularly when a high proportion of recruits for the British Army fighting the Boer War were found to be in very poor physical condition and the Report of an Inter-Departmental Committee on this problem was published in 1904[1]. In 1906 Parliament passed the Education (Provision of Meals) Act which empowered local authorities to provide milk and meals to children in their schools if the children were unable by reason of lack of food to take full advantage of the education provided for them. In 1907 the Education (Administrative Provisions) Act created a School Medical Service. A Medical Department of the Board of Education was set up and the regular medical inspection of school children was authorised. Curiously, however, the Act did not provide for medical treatment: this was authorised in 1912. As with so many other Acts of Parliament in the period 1870 to 1914, a good deal once again depended on the degree of local enthusiasm and initiative: some local authorities appeared to be very half-hearted, but a few were so keen that they went so far as to prosecute parents who, after due warning, persisted in sending their children to school with lice in their hair.

The success of Acts of Parliament such as those mentioned above also depended on the numbers and skill of trained medical personnel. Fortunately, the number of doctors in Britain increased from 15,000 in 1881 to 22,000 in 1901. At the same time medical training had been put on a more systematic basis, a joint examination in medicine and surgery having been introduced by the Royal Colleges in 1886.

A proportion of doctors went into local government service, of course. They were often men of great energy and initiative, and in their work they were encouraged by such powerful figures as John Simon, the Chief Medical Officer of the Local Government Board. Their work benefited, too, from the support of other local officials:

---

[1] The story goes that a young recruit, turned down because of rotten teeth, complained that he wanted to fight the Boers, not bite them!

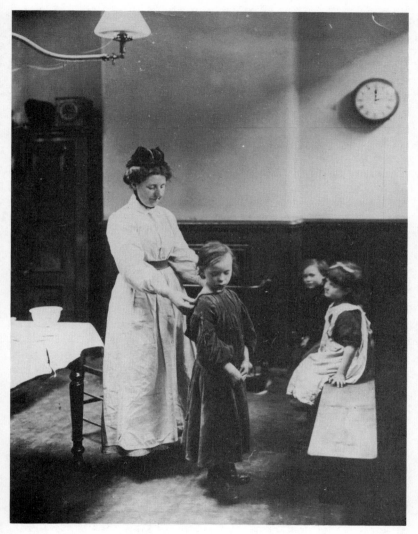

School medical inspection, 1912

in 1883 the Association of Public Health Inspectors was founded and in 1901 the Association of Managers of Sewage Disposal Works.

Hospitals, too, benefited from the development of the medical profession. In 1860 the Nightingale School of Nursing was opened at St. Thomas' Hospital, London, and gradually the trained nurse made her impact. The training put an immense emphasis on cleanliness, care and devotion, preparing the trainees for what was bound to be a long and hard fight against squalor and callousness in many British hospitals. The real breakthrough came, perhaps, in the Poor Law Infirmaries, where it had been the custom to employ female paupers as nurses. In 1865, for instance, when Agnes Jones went to Brownlow Hill Infirmary she found that bedclothes were often unwashed for months. Yet in the 1890's, George Lansbury, a pioneer Socialist and strong opponent of the Poor Law, willingly admitted that workhouse hospitals were 'vastly improved', especially in respect of cleanliness.

The demand for trained nurses became, in fact, very great, especially when the use of paupers was forbidden by law in 1877. Between 1881 and 1901 total numbers in the nursing profession rose from 38,000 to 68,000.

At this period the building of new hospitals, and the improvement of old, was financed by great funds such as the Hospital Sunday funds, and by an increased willingness to use money from the rates for this purpose. By 1900 the total number of hospitals had risen and included 600 cottage hospitals. New specialised occupations appeared: the Institute of Hospital Administrators was established in 1902; the Hospital Almoners' Association was founded in 1903; the Institute of Medical Laboratory Technology was founded in 1912.

Within hospitals generally a number of overall improvements were made. Patients with infectious diseases were kept apart from other patients; antiseptic measures pioneered by Lister in the 1860's were gradually adopted; specialist anaesthetists appeared, and local anaesthetics for dental surgery were increasingly used in the 1890's. After opposition in some hospitals, internal telephone systems were instituted; electric lighting appeared after 1904. Distinctive uniforms for the different grades of nurses were introduced.

Medical science itself made conspicuous advances in this period, although much of the significance of these advances was to be in the future. Often, indeed, medical discoveries were slow to 'catch on': it was not, for instance, until 1890 that John Simon came fully to accept the germ theory of disease. Yet *scientific* break-throughs were made. In 1895 Rontgen discovered X rays; in 1898 the Curies isolated radium; in 1902 a Frenchman called Alexis Carrel published a paper showing how major blood vessels could be joined and went on to experiment with the transplanting of organs in animals; the disciples of Pasteur worked on producing vaccines, and in 1913 a German called Emil von Behring pioneered mass diphtheria immunisation. Already, as we have seen, the first vitamin had been isolated. In a sense the way had been paved for the great step forward in medical science that was to take place after the First World War.

Social Security

It has been pointed out that one of the main features that made the nineteenth century different from the twentieth was the huge volume of poverty which existed in the former period. Perhaps, however, this is an over-simplification. Perhaps, indeed, it was not so much the actual amount of poverty but the wider *fear* of poverty that was the more important factor.

Three things seem to have been of special significance here: the inability of the ordinary family to protect itself against misfortune, the frequent trade depressions that threw men out of work, and the real horrors of being a pauper.

Now, in spite of the large numbers of sick clubs and benefit societies to which many of the poorer classes belonged, the capacity of the average working class family to save so as to protect its members against sickness, unemployment and old age was very limited. In 1882 it was calculated that wages in London averaged below £1 per week. Yet the rent of three unfurnished rooms was 7s 6d (37½p). Charles Booth worked out that a family of father, mother and three children needed £1 1s 7d (£1.08) per week to live in such a way that they could maintain their health. Yet other investigations showed that, in York, at least, one family out of every ten fell below these standards.

When unemployment came a man, however honest and sober

Bradford 1900; like all British cities contained much poverty

he might be, could quickly reach a state of desperation. Will Crooks, a London cooper who later became an M.P., later described his own experience: 'I went down to the river-side at Shadwell. No hands wanted. So I looked in at home and got two slices of bread in paper and walked eight miles to a cooper's yard in Tottenham. All in vain. I dragged myself back to Clerkenwell. Still no luck. Then I turned towards home in despair. By the time I reached Stepney I was dead beat, so I called at a friend's in Commercial Road for a little rest. They gave me some Irish stew and two pence to ride home. I managed to walk home and gave the two pence to my wife. She needed it badly.'

The plight of the old was even sadder, for an improvement in trade was usually meaningless to them. Charles Booth in his *Pauperism and the Endowment of Old Age* (1892) graphically described the plight of old people, half-starving but terrified of the workhouse: 'where out-relief is withheld, and especially in towns, we find numbers of people struggling on, working a little, begging a little, helped by their friends or helped by the church; people who would be glad to accept poor relief if given outside, but who manage to keep above ground somewhere by these other means if out-relief is denied. . . . Such people probably live in greater discomfort than those who frankly accept pauperism.'

Fear of the workhouse was, in fact, very great—a fear not so much of its harshness but of its degradation. Paupers in a real sense ceased to be members of society: as the Webbs pointed out, they were sent to 'gaols without guilt'. George Lansbury described a visit to a workhouse in the 1890's: 'Going down a narrow lane, ringing the bell, waiting while an official with a not too pleasant face looked through a grating to see who was there, and hearing his unpleasant voice . . . made it easy for me to understand why the poor dreaded and hated these places.'

Some improvement, it is true, was made between 1870 and 1900. Standards of cleanliness, especially in workhouse hospitals, were raised. Joseph Chamberlain secured the vote at least for 'medical' paupers. By the Local Government Act of 1894 women and working men became eligible for election as Poor Law Guardians administering the system locally, and this strengthened the position of individuals such as George Lansbury and Will Crooks who were campaigning for better conditions. Standards of education, especially among senior staff, rose and 'promotion ladders' were introduced. Sheffield began to experiment with a 'scattered home' system, the forerunner of the modern family group house.

On the other hand, little would have been achieved had there not been a growing acceptance of *the idea* that simply to deter was not enough. In other words, there was a growing realisation that people could be destitute through no fault of their own and that poverty could not be overcome by punishing, as it were, those who became destitute. As David Lloyd George said in respect of unemployment, 'the workman is the least to blame . . . he is not responsible, although he bears almost all the real privation.' The same was true of most of those who were poor by reason of old age.

In 1908 the Budget made provision for the payment of Old Age Pensions. The scheme, it is interesting to note, has always been associated with the name of Lloyd George: indeed it was not unusual for an old person in the years which followed the passing of the Act to refer to his pension as his 'Lloyd George'. On the other hand, it should be remembered that the fiery Welshman took over responsibility for the Budget only at a late stage when it already included the pension proposals. It should also be remembered that the idea owed a good deal to Charles Booth (who had calculated that old age accounted for 32·8 per cent of poverty) to Sidney and

Beatrice Webb and to the Report of a Royal Commission on the Aged Poor which had sat in 1895. Nevertheless, it was David Lloyd George who, in his Limehouse Speech of July 1909, gave what was perhaps the most moving justification of the step that had been taken: 'It is rather hard that an old workman should have to find his way to the gates of the tomb, bleeding and footsore, through the branches and thorns of poverty. We cut a new path through it, an easier one, through fields of waving corn. We are raising money to pay for this new road, aye, and to widen it so that two hundred thousand paupers shall be able to join in the march.'

The pensions, which were to be paid at post offices, were non-contributory. The Government had, in fact, turned down the idea of contributory pensions (that is, pensions paid for out of deductions from wages) because such a scheme would have taken at least twenty years to come into operation. The Act applied to more than 500,000 people, providing a maximum pension of 5s (25p) per week to an individual and 7s 6d (37½p) per week to a married couple. Persons below a certain income level, qualified for the pension at the age of seventy, although individuals could be disqualified if they had shown evidence of lazy or criminal habits. The pension was not

The first Old Age Pensioners,
1909

enough to live on (nor was it intended to be), but with small savings, earnings or family help it succeeded in keeping large numbers out of the workhouse or the pathetic, grinding poverty that had been the alternative.

The problem of the unemployed workman remained, although some protection against the results of industrial injury had been given by the Workmen's (Compensation for Accidents) Bill of 1894, coming at a time when only 12 men in every 100 injured in industrial accidents received any form of compensation. Unfortunately, lack of clarity in the wording of the Act had caused long legal delays, a situation that was not entirely remedied by the Workmen's Compensation Act of 1906.

The Unemployed Workmen's Act of 1905 gave the Local Government Board power to establish unemployment committees to keep registers of local unemployed and to set up labour exchanges. Unfortunately, these committees could not give financial assistance to the unemployed and in this and other ways the Act was quite unsatisfactory.

In 1909, however, William H. Beveridge published his *Unemployment, a Problem of Industry* and in the same year came The Labour Exchanges Act. The exchanges, which were designed to make employment vacancies known to men who were unemployed or who wished to change their jobs, were to be staffed by civil servants and 250 were established, some with special juvenile departments. In 1910 the Education (Choice of Employment) Act compelled local authorities to provide a service for young people under seventeen years of age with the help of supervision and a grant from the Board of Education.

In 1911 the National Insurance Act was passed. All workers between the ages of 16 and 70 who earned £160 per year or less were to be insured. Unlike the Old Age Pensions, this was to be a contributory scheme. To finance the scheme both worker and employer made weekly contributions: a grant from the state was added. The fund was used to provide sickness pay and 'panel' doctors and medicine when a worker fell ill. As a system it functioned with little change up to 1948.

A beginning was made at the same time with unemployment insurance. The scheme was worked through 'approved societies', which could be friendly societies, trade unions or insurance companies. Once again, however, the three-fold system of payment (employee, employer and state) was used. The funds thus created were to be used to support a person who was temporarily out of work. At first, however, the scheme was restricted to eight 'precarious' trades (such as building and ship-building), so that the drain on funds would not be too great should there be a general slump in trade. In these circumstances only 2·25 million men, or one-sixth of the working population, was covered at first. Initially, 7s (35p) in unemployment pay could be paid. This was the famous 'dole'.

All in all it would be wrong either to ignore the advances made in social security between 1870 and 1914 or to exaggerate them. In 1913 the total Government contribution to the cost of pensions, sickness and unemployment benefits and labour exchanges was only one per cent of the national income. Perhaps the real turning point had come with the development of a more humane attitude to the unfortunate in society.

Leisure

By modern standards, as we have seen, leisure time for working people tended to be limited in the period 1870–1914. Some improvement came, it is true. In 1871 an Act of Parliament established Bank Holidays on Boxing Day, Easter and Whit-Monday and the first Monday in August. By 1900 Saturday half-holidays were fairly general. On the other hand, daily hours still tended to remain long. As late as 1894, for instance, a survey of 206 occupations showed that in the case of 142, or nearly 70 per cent, a 10-hour day (with Sundays and one afternoon off) was being worked.

By 1875, however, some of the better paid office workers had been given two or even three weeks' holiday, and in some cases this was with pay. What is thought to be the first instance of paid holidays for manual workers came in 1884 when the firm of Brunner-Mond gave some of its employees an annual week's holiday with pay.

What is certain is that holidays became more customary at this period. This development was, in part, stimulated by the increasing efficiency and comfort of the railways. The following figures tell their own story:

Year	Miles of Rail Open	Passengers carried
1871	13,388 miles (21,566 km)	359·7 million
1891	17,328 miles (27,886 km)	823·3 million
1911	20,015 miles (32,211 km)	1,295·5 million

Throughout the nineteenth century there was a trend towards the development of heavier and more powerful railway engines. By the 1890's some engines, such as those of the Atlantic class, weighed more than 100 tonnes apiece. This allowed for longer coaches with more wheels and improved suspension. Electric lighting from batteries or dynamos began to be introduced, and side corridors and lavatories appeared. In 1874 Pullman cars were brought on, bringing with them new standards in service and comfort. For longer journeys dining cars and sleeping cars were welcome innovations.

Of special importance to the less wealthy traveller, however, was the improvement of the third class, an improvement which led gradually to the disappearance of the old second class. In 1891 the Great Western Railway Company introduced the through corridor train, and at roughly this time the Midland Railway Company established heating and padded seats in third class compartments.

A children's seaside trip, 1913

With such services the day by the seaside, with its roundabouts, Punch and Judy shows and pier performances, became increasingly popular. Blackpool was already a town by 1876 and subsequently day trips in the West extended to the Isle of Man. It is interesting to note that the 1871 census listed 48 seaside resorts, but by 1901 another 15 had been added and these included Bournemouth, Paignton and Skegness.

Nor were seaside resorts the only object of day trips. The Crystal Palace was transferred from its original home to Beckenham, where its attractions included a zoo. A day trip to such a place could be an exciting adventure for a child, especially when unexpected events took place. In 1900, for instance, Charlie the elephant escaped and wrecked a number of gardens before being recaptured.

For more and more people a week or more by the seaside was becoming a possibility, and the effect of this on some seaside towns was dramatic. Torquay grew in population from 21,657 in 1871 to 33,625 in 1907, Bournemouth from 5,896 to 47,003 in the same period. The Isle of Wight also became popular. Eye-witness accounts of this period depict well-to-do travellers travelling to holiday there with their children, nannies, baggage, prams and bath tubs—a remarkable feat of family organisation.

Meanwhile, the rich had tended to desert inland spas such as Buxton, Harrogate and Cheltenham for foreign watering places. The famous travel firm of Thomas Cook introduced tours of the Middle East in 1869 and by 1872 was advertising a round-the-world tour. In 1913 over 750,000 Britons left the country for Europe, most of them middle-class tourists going on holiday.

For those who stayed at home the development of the bicycle made possible the exploration of an English countryside that was becoming gradually more appreciated. The change from earlier attitudes was interesting. In the eighteenth century the Peak District had been described as 'a howling wilderness': in the twentieth century its beauty was to make it Britain's first National Park. In 1895 the National Trust had been founded to buy and protect places of great natural beauty.

The cycle, which really came into its own in the 1890's, was, in fact, significant in a number of ways. Its use helped to encourage the wearing of less cumbersome clothes by women and girls—at a time when people dressed very carefully for sea-bathing and lady tennis players were not encouraged to *run* after the ball! The bicycle's capacity to carry loads also encouraged the sport of camping. In August 1901 the Association of Cycle Campers, the forerunner of the modern Camping Club of Great Britain and Ireland, was founded. In 1904, it is recorded, nine hardy souls attended a Christmas Camp.

Not that cycling was without its dangers. The bone-shaker of the 1860's, the penny farthing of the 70's and the later 'safety bicycle' all represented advance, as did the pneumatic tyre patented

A farmworkers' trip to Yarmouth, 1906

in 1888 by J. B. Dunlop, an Irish veterinary surgeon who had never actually ridden a bicycle, but wished his son, Johnnie, to win a race against bigger boys. Yet two entries in *The Sheffield Local Register* for 1901 tell their own story:

> 'June 4th. A Sheffield lady named Miss Kate Scott, of 130 Steade Road, meets with a terrible cycling accident whilst riding down the Cupola into Baslow.
> 'June 5th. A youth named Bertram Norman, of 93 Pyebank, loses control of his cycle near Fox House and collides with the "Old Times Coach", seriously injuring himself.'

For the rich the recently-invented motor car provided a new mode of travel. At first, however, and for some years, cars were little more than 'playthings of the rich'. Dr. Otto invented the first internal combustion engine in 1876; the first light engined car appeared in 1887; the British law which required self-propelled vehicles to be preceded by a man with a red flag was repealed in 1896. Yet in 1901 only 623 males were listed in Britain as having the occupation of motor car driver.

In 1903, however, when the Motor Car Act required motor vehicles to be licensed, 18,000 were registered in twelve months. In 1909 a petrol tax of 3d (1½p) per gallon (4·5 litre) was introduced.

As might have been expected, motor car travelling before the First World War had its discomforts and hazards. The rubber tyres raised great clouds of dust from roads until tar was used to bind the surface. There were, of course, no garages as such: petrol was sold in 2-gallon (9-litre) drums by ironmongers and cycle shops and repairs were done by blacksmiths. Motorists were often represented as boastful and selfish people, rather like the character of Toad in *The Wind in the Willows*. Even between 1899 and 1903 traffic offences averaged some 1,600 per year!

If new pleasures were being introduced—and it is interesting that cinema-going had increased to such an extent that it was thought necessary in 1909 for Parliament to pass an Act enforcing fire regulations in picture houses[1]—old pleasures continued to develop. The fair continued to hold its attraction, such as the one at Battersea Fields, with its '60–120 horses and donkeys racing, foot-races, walking matches, flying boats, flying horses, roundabouts, theatres, actors, shameless dancers, conjurers, fortune tellers, gambles of every description, drinking booths, stalls, hawkers and vendors of all kinds of articles'.

The period 1870 to 1914 saw a movement towards the mass sport of the modern period. There were some events such as the Derby which had a long history, as had the still-popular sport of long-distance walking which opened a new chapter in 1878 when Sir John Astley introduced the six-day 'Go as You Please' contests, immense tests of stamina in which distances of 600 miles (965 km) or more were recorded. On the other hand, this was the period in which the great modern football clubs had their origin and the Football Association was founded. An account of a football match in Sheffield in 1875, which was seen by 3,000 people, has a curiously modern ring about it:

> 'The electric light was thrown from four arc lamps 30 feet from the ground, and the rays, which were of the greatest brilliancy, lighted the whole of the ground, the players being seen almost as clearly as at noonday. The brilliancy of the light, however, dazzled the players, and sometimes caused strange blunders. The illuminating power was equal to 8,000 candles.'

The period 1870 to 1914 was also, in a very real sense, the golden age of the gas-lit music halls. In London halls such as the Empire and the Tivoli could seat more than 1,000, with prices from 6d (2½p) to 9d (4p). There were many imitations in provincial towns. These were lavishly decorated and well-furnished: places where men could bring their wives. They had their 'stars'—Vesta Tilley, Little Titch, Dan Leno, Marie Lloyd—and their songs which were to be heard later in the trenches and billets of soldiers in the First World

---

[1] Motion pictures, in crude form, can be traced back to 1894.

A football match in 1888

War. The music hall tended to drive out the melodrama and the long comic sketch on which the earlier theatre had thrived: it was later to suffer savage competition from the cinema.

For those who enjoyed quieter pleasures, the period saw a great development in materials for reading. The removal of stamp duties on newspapers encouraged the improvement of local newspapers, some of which, like *The Yorkshire Post*, were to become very famous. The improvement in the education of even poor people also stimulated the appearance of popular magazines, with short, interesting stories, puzzles and prizes. In 1881 *Titbits* appeared, and by 1892 Alfred Harmsworth (later Lord Northcliffe) was selling 300,000 weekly copies of *Answers*, with articles on such topics as 'What the Queen Eats' and 'How to Cure Freckles'. Newspaper 'giants' such as *The Daily Mail* and *The Daily Express* appeared.

Nor was the increase in reading matter for adults only. This was the age when the magic story of *Alice in Wonderland* appeared and the exciting adventure stories of Captain Marryat and Ballantyne were published.

In other ways, too, the increase in leisure and basic education produced new ways of developing minds and bodies. By 1913 the Workers' Educational Association, originally founded as 'an Association to Promote the Higher Education of Working Men' had 11,000 members. Meanwhile, the Church Lads' Brigade and the Boy Scouts had been founded.

Such were some of the main ways in which the use of leisure developed in the period 1870–1914. The economic advance which in many respects created the problems which have been discussed in the earlier chapters, at the same time allowed many people to enjoy a fuller life, in which leisure played an increasing part.

The Middle Classes

Much of this book is concerned with the life of the mass of the people of Britain in the last century or so. It may seem very strange, therefore, that one section of the nation should be singled out for special investigation. This is done for two reasons. First, because social class differences were very wide, particularly in the nineteenth century: it is difficult, as Disraeli had complained, to write of 'the British people'. Secondly, because in many ways the middle class, and again particularly in the nineteenth century, has represented ideas which were very important in society as a whole.

Between 1870 and 1914 there was a considerable increase in the number of families with incomes of £200 per annum or above. In days of low taxation incomes such as these guaranteed a good standard of living for the recipients. In 1899, for instance, Seebohm Rowntree found that 29 per cent of the population of York kept at least one living-in servant.

In the later twentieth century the domestic servant is, of course, a comparative rarity. Yet there is still in existence evidence of the wealth of the middle classes before the First World War. This evidence includes the church buildings that were built with their

A group of domestic servants about 1890

donations and the great Victorian dwelling houses, solidly built of good red brick, often with turrets, pinnacles and other decorations. The great hotels of that time also continue to exist in some of our cities. Their lavish entrance halls and large rooms still give some idea of the comfort in which the well-to-do expected to live in those times.

This, then, was a class that was growing in wealth and numbers. There were still fortunes to be made in business and industry, and a fair proportion of middle-class fathers came into the category of 'self-made men', men who were generally eager that their sons should have the best possible education and come to be regarded as 'gentlemen'. Often fun was poked at such people by individuals who had been born into the middle class: Trollope's *The Way We Live Now*, published in 1875, was an example of this some-what unkind attitude. Other elements came into the middle class as the professions expanded. Between 1881 and 1901, for instance, the numbers of those employed in government and administration rose by 70,000. The increasing number of professional qualifications at this period gave a new type of stratum in society.

Although it is difficult to generalise, it is broadly true to say that the middle classes of Victorian and Edwardian Britain took a pride in their wealth. This was reflected in the crowding of their rooms with possessions and the heavy ornamentation of their furniture. Even the spacious rooms of a Victorian house, with its sofas, mantelpiece clocks, bird cages, pianos, pictures, potted plants and so on, would seem hopelessly overcrowded to the modern eye.

There was also in the middle classes in general a deeply felt belief in the merits of hard work and self-discipline. It has been pointed out that this was an age when the average middle-class family went out very little. This explains, of course, the importance attached to music lessons in this period and the large sales of sheet music: the musical evening at home was, of course, very popular.

The middle classes, too, were major supporters of the churches in the nineteenth century. Private pews were not unknown, even at the end of the century, and it is perhaps not surprising that it was the chapels which attracted working men and women and that organisations such as the Salvation Army and the East London missions came into existence to 'take religion to the people'. Meanwhile, for the average middle-class family, sermons and Sundays loomed large. Even the walk to and from church was important, with the father leading the way and the womenfolk following with velvet-covered prayer books.

Perhaps, too, it is true to say that the middle classes had their fair share of confidence in Britain and things British which characterised the age. This was, after all, an age in which Joseph Chamberlain, a self-made manufacturer of screws, could become a leading figure in British politics. This was also the age of the music hall song, 'We don't want to fight, but by jingo if we do . . .' and the verse:

> 'England, England, England
> Girded by oceans and skies,
> And the power of the world,
> And the heart of a race,
> And a hope that never dies.'

It is true that the publication of Darwin's *Origin of Species* had to some extent shaken faith in the literal truth of the Old Testament and that recurring slumps after 1870 and the growth of foreign competition could not be ignored. Yet Britain remained strong.

Stability certainly existed in the middle class, but it could not entirely hide change. The family firm was to some extent giving way to the larger firm professionally run by salaried managers. The numbers of professional men were increasing at a time when increasingly qualification depended on the passing of examinations. There was a slight but growing emphasis on leisure as golf, tennis and cricket became more popular and rock-climbing came into its own.

Clerical workers of the City of London, 1914

Perhaps most important of all, however, was the gradual change in attitude to middle-class women. In the early nineteenth century the middle-class wife and daughter had been regarded very much in terms of what today would be thought of as 'status symbols'. The wife of a businessman, for instance, had little to do but to supervise the servants. Even the bringing up of small children was customarily left to nannies.

For an intelligent young woman the situation could be one of great frustration. In 1894 one such young woman complained: 'A daughter must arrange the flowers, help with the housekeeping, pay the family calls, entertain the family visitors, always be at hand, well-dressed, cheerful and smiling . . . *She can never undertake any definite work or pursuit.*'

Yet things were slowly changing in a variety of ways. In 1887, for instance, a shocked writer in *The Birmingham Gazette* related how 'three young ladies entered a railway carriage and proceeded to light cigarettes in public . . . the calm audacity of the proceedings showed that the girls, though young, were practised smokers.'

More seriously, there was some progress in women's education and their entry into responsible jobs. The Girls' Public Day School Trust opened 33 schools between 1872 and 1900. Girton College, Cambridge, opened in 1869 (although Cambridge degrees were not awarded to women until the 1920's). Women's colleges were established at Oxford and London Universities.

Gradually women penetrated public life. They were, for instance, allowed to sit on the School Boards established by the Education Act of 1870. By 1900 Sheffield had appointed a woman sanitary inspector. In 1881 there were only 25 women doctors in Britain: by 1901 there were 212. There were 100 women law clerks in 1881: by 1901 there were 367. There were three women architects recorded in 1901, but there were no women barristers or solicitors. For other women, as we have seen in another chapter, the development of office work, government services and the communication industry offered increased employment opportunities. Even so, in 1901 there were 9,018,000 women without employment and of these only some six million or so were married.

Gradual progress was being made too in the improvement of the legal status of women. An Act of 1870, for instance, allowed a married woman to retain her own earnings. A series of Married Women's Property Acts ensured that a married woman's property was not automatically to be regarded as that of her husband. Gradually, in fact, the enormous power that the Victorian husband had over his wife was whittled away, partly by changes in the law and partly by changes in attitude. In 1878 F. P. Cobb in his book *Wife Torture* suggested the idea of legal separation when a marriage was unhappy but when divorce was not available.

The question of votes for women inevitably came up. There was considerable opposition to this and in 1903 the Women's Social and Political Union, in which the Pankhursts were to play a leading role, was formed. When peaceful demonstrations failed, violence erupted. Women chained themselves to railings, pictures in galleries

A Suffragette meeting, 1912

were slashed, the royal horse was brought down in the Derby in an incident in which a 'suffragette' was killed. When suffragettes were imprisoned they might well go on hunger strike. There was fear that death might result and in 1913 the notorious 'Cat and Mouse' Act was passed by Parliament whereby a woman prisoner might be released but imprisoned again when her health had improved. The outbreak of war in 1914 brought such things to an end and the subsequent shortage of labour allowed women to prove conclusively that they could undertake work and shoulder responsibilities that had hitherto been considered suitable only for men. The day of the 'Bird in the Gilded Cage' (to quote an old song) had come to an end.

Finding Out About Society

Although it is fairly easy to grasp the main changes in British society between 1870 and 1914, it would be wrong to assume that the people who lived at the time had a complete and accurate picture of the Britain in which they lived. The nineteenth century was, in fact, an age of considerable social ignorance. When, for instance, the famous Sanitary Report of 1842 was published it was said that people of the time read it as though about some far-off foreign country.

The securing of accurate information was thus an activity of considerable importance. To some extent this was the work of the new army of officials which appeared in the nineteenth century, the Inspectors of Schools, the Medical Officers of Health, the Inspectors of Constabulary and so on. The Census Returns and the famous *Blue Books* published officially also contained a mass of information.

Sometimes the information could be very graphic indeed. In the early 1890's for instance, Sir Robert Giffen, the Permanent Secretary to the Board of Trade, reported to a Royal Commission on Labour that in 1885 23 per cent of adult workers earned £1 per week or less.

Yet, in many ways, it was the private investigators whose finds were the most influential in shaping public opinion. Among these was Charles Booth, a wealthy Liverpool ship-owner who in 1903 completed the seventeenth volume of his *Life and Labour of the People of London*.

Booth was very much impressed by the scientific achievement of the nineteenth century and wished to make his investigation as 'scientific' as he possibly could. He began his work in Tower Hamlets in the East End of London in the 1880's, and his work was described as 'the grimmest book of our generation'. His conclusion was that one-third of the population of London were 'sinking into want'. In general his evidence was supported by the investigations of Scott in Manchester.

Another great and influential investigator was Seebohm Rowntree, a man who knew Booth personally and built on his experience. Rowntree's *Poverty: a Study of Town Life* was published in 1901 and was an intensive study of York, where the Quaker Rowntree family were well-established chocolate and cocoa manufacturers. Rowntree's study profited from the fact that he was able to get information *direct* from working-class families.

Like Booth, Rowntree strove after scientific accuracy. In particular he wished to establish a more precise definition of poverty and for this purpose worked out a minimum figure based on the cost of food, clothing, fuel and rent for a family of a given size. For instance, he worked out that a family of five needed £1 1s 7d (£1.08) if it was not to fall below his 'poverty' line.

Rowntree also analysed the causes of the poverty dealt with in his study:

1	Regular work, but low wages	51·96%
2	Size of family (four children or more)	22·16%
3	Death of chief wage-earner	15·63%
4	Old age or illness of chief wage-earner	5·11%
5	Irregularity of work	2·83%
6	Unemployment of chief wage-earner	2·31%

In spite of the fact that York was considered to be relatively prosperous, Rowntree's report presented a grim picture. His conclusion was blunt: 'We are faced with the startling probability that from 25 per cent to 30 per cent of the town populations of the United Kingdom are living in poverty.'

Here, then, was a troubling picture of malnutrition and squalor. According to Booth, three out of every ten people in

A beggar in London, 1874

London lived in overcrowded, squalid houses. As in almost every other aspect of British life, many families were being left behind in the *general* improvement described in other sections of this book. The evidence, it will be noted, was confirmed by other writers, including General William Booth, the founder of the Salvation Army, who in 1890 published *In Darkest England and the Way Out*, a book which made the surprising assertion that in England many honest working men were worse off than convicts.

The urge to find out continued and methods of investigation became increasingly scientific. There were surveys of West Ham in 1907, Middlesbrough in 1907 and Norwich in 1910. In 1914 A. L. Bowley and A. R. Burnett-Hurst made a study of five towns using the technique of sampling.

Meanwhile, important evidence had come from another source. Published figures showed that in 1900 infant mortality in Britain stood at about 160 deaths per 1,000. This, however, was less striking than the fact that a large proportion of young men who tried to join the army at this time were found to be unfit.

In 1904 the *Report on Physical Deterioration* was published, and this showed that between 1893 and 1902 some 35 per cent of the recruits considered for the armed forces were rejected after initial inspection, another one per cent was rejected within the next three

A Sunderland slum, 1889

months and a further two per cent were dismissed during their first year in the army. These facts, together with some of the other evidence mentioned in this chapter, led Sir Frederick Maurice, the Inspector-General of Recruiting, to suggest that if a European war broke out as many as one in every three men of military age in Britain would be unfit for service in the armed forces. This was a frightening prospect for the nation—especially in the years when hostility developed between Britain and Germany and both nations took part in a race to see who could build the biggest and best battleships.[1]

   One important result of all this social investigation was social reform. Some of this was the work of determined individuals. Among these were Rachel and Margaret McMillan, sisters who in town streets found children who were 'half naked, unwashed, and covered in sores'. In 1908 they were able to open a school clinic in the London area of Bow.

   By this time, however, it had come to be more widely accepted that the nation itself must take steps to overcome the great mass of poverty, ill health and unhappiness to which its attention had been drawn. The result was a great rush of 'social legislation' in the years between 1900 and 1914. Much of this legislation is described in other chapters of this book, but it is useful to summarise

[1] It is also interesting to note that when war did break out in 1914, and soldiers came from Australia and New Zealand their greater average physical size compared with that of their counterparts from British towns was much commented on.

it here as evidence of the great impact which the work of scientific social investigation had on our society in the early years of the twentieth century.

In 1905 a Liberal Government came to power and began to carry through a wide range of reforms. Indeed these reforms were so far-reaching that many people consider that, in a real sense, they laid the basis of the Welfare State that we know today.

In 1906 local councils were given powers to provide school meals for the children of poor families. School medical inspection was begun in 1907. In 1908 the Children's Act protected children in a number of ways—e.g. by keeping them out of public houses and by prohibiting the imprisonment of children under 14.

In 1908, too, came Old Age Pensions, together with a Coal Mines Act, that, among other things, fixed a maximum working day for miners in that industry. In 1909 the Trades Boards Act, which was partly the direct result of Charles Booth's investigations in London, fixed minimum wages in a number of notoriously badly paid trades such as tailoring. Labour Exchanges were also created in 1909, and in 1911 came National Insurance and the Shops Act, the latter securing a weekly half-holiday for shop assistants.

These, then, were the results of the investigations described in the first part of this chapter. The fundamental point was, of course, that a new attitude to social reform had gradually developed. Poverty, bad health, ignorance, distress—these were no longer problems which could either be ignored or accepted as inevitable. There was now earnest discussion of what the 'national minimum standard of life', beneath which no one should be allowed to fall, should be, and also of ways of providing 'social security'. Further progress along these lines is described in later chapters.

The Land

Between 1870 and 1914 there was a sharp fall in the proportion of the country's labour force employed on the land. Between 1875 and 1890 alone this exodus involved something like a third of the rural population.

One factor in all this was the competition from imports of foreign food. By 1914 something like 50 per cent of the country's food requirements came from abroad. As we have seen in an earlier chapter, these imports enriched the nation's diet, but they also were to make the country vulnerable to submarine warfare in the two World Wars of the twentieth century.

The effect on the nature of the British countryside and its life varied from area to area. In general, the light soils of East Anglia and the South-East competed most successfully whilst the heavier soils elsewhere competed less well, particularly against imports of foreign grain. Over the country as a whole there was a change-over to pastoral farming. In 1867 there were about 3·3 million acres (1·3 million hectares) of land devoted to the production of wheat in Great Britain; by 1913 the figure had fallen to something like 1·75 million acres (700,000 hectares). On the other hand cattle numbers rose from about 5 million in 1870 to some 7 million in 1913. This development, it will be noted, had been encouraged by increased imports of cattle foodstuffs such as maize and cotton-seed cake.

The swing to pasture farming was associated with a fall in the numbers of people living in the countryside. It is easy to see why this should be so. *The Report on Women's and Children's Employment* (1867) calculated that arable mixed farming required one man for every 25 or 30 acres (10 or 12 hectares), whereas pasture farming required only one man for every 50 or 60 acres (20 or 24 hectares). Coming at a time when the use of machinery was being developed on some farms, though not all (reaping by sickle was not unknown, even in 1900) the extension of pasture farming produced a fall in the demand for labour.

It should be remembered, too, that not all the workers who left the countryside were small farmers and labourers. The numbers of rural craftsmen and small traders diminished. The blacksmith, carpenter, wheelwright, goods carrier and small shopkeeper also suffered from a fall in the demand for their services. Between 1881 and 1901 the number of veterinary surgeons fell from some 7,000 to 3,000 in the country as a whole.

In some areas, though not all, the effect was profound. An extreme example of the changes that could take place was the little village of Snape in Wiltshire. In the nineteenth century there was a chapel, cottages and a little school attended by 44 children. In 1921 it was mere ruins in grassland.

Other developments affected the British countryside and its life. In country areas of Durham, Yorkshire, Nottinghamshire, Lancashire and South Wales the pithead and the massive tip appeared more frequently. Indeed the huge increase in mining (in some areas the mining labour force doubled between 1881 and 1901, and a new record for coal production was reached in 1913) was made possible only by the erosion of the countryside.

Another big change was the expansion of market gardening and fruit growing. As the towns continued to grow, the demand for fresh food increased. Small-scale, highly intensive cultivation took place. Artificial fertilisers were brought in to supplement the huge amounts of manure from the towns, plant diseases were reduced by the introduction of spraying, and improved types of seed were developed. The practice of boxing seeds and planting sprouting sets also became more customary.

An additional development was the creation of larger farms with larger fields. Small farms represented one-fifth of the land in the early part of the nineteenth century: by 1900 they represented merely one-eighth. As the small farms fell in numbers there was a

A piece of late 19th century farm machinery

tendency to consolidate the larger units. Generally speaking, it was
the large-scale land-owner who had the capital to carry him through
the bad years and the resources to invest in the machinery, such
as the self-acting binder which made its mark in the 1880's. To use
such machinery economically required larger fields, however, and so
the process of removing old hedges and walls continued, and indeed
continues in some areas in present-day farming.

And what of the people who lived in the countryside? For
the 'middling' farmer these were not, on the whole, good years, and
the problem of 'getting British agriculture back on its feet' was to be
an important one for the people of the twentieth century to tackle.
According to Sir James Laird's evidence before a Royal
Commission, there was a fall in agricultural incomes of some £43
million between 1876 and 1886. Some help, it is true, came from

Parliament in the nineteenth century, but not a great deal was done effectively to prevent low returns, a general fall-off in standards of hedging and ditching and the reversion of good agricultural land to rough pasture. A Minister of Agriculture was appointed in 1889, but a Royal Commission's Report of 1893 was of a troubling nature. Subsequently, the Agricultural Rates Act of 1896 provided for relief from rates in cases of hardship, whilst an Improvement of Land Act increased facilities for carrying out improvements on land using borrowed money.

The owner of very large estates, however, appears to have withstood the strains more successfully, especially when his income was increased by house rents and the royalties from coal mines and similar industrial enterprises. The great agricultural shows continued to prosper, the opulent country house party remained a feature of upper class life, and further progress was made in the breeding of superb herds of pedigree cattle. Large estates were also the first to benefit from the training of experts in the agricultural colleges which appeared in the 1890's.

In many ways, too, the *general* lot of the farm worker appears to have improved between 1870 and 1914, although there were always many individual cases of poverty and hardship.

Early attempts at trade union organisation appeared to achieve little. Joseph Arch's trade union, founded at Wellesbourne in February 1872, after Arch, a Nonconformist local preacher, had addressed a group of labourers under an oak tree, enrolled 150,000 members but weakened under severe pressure. There were other attempts to form unions in the 1880's and 1890's but it was not until 1906 that the National Union of Agricultural Workers was formed, initially in the Eastern Counties, and a campaign was waged for a Parliamentary Bill to establish minimum wages.

Meanwhile, an increasing shortage of labour seems to have helped the cause of the farm labourer to some extent. Workers tended to leave the countryside because they wanted better wages, because they resented the system of 'tied' cottages whereby a man who lost his job lost his home as well and because they deprecated the essentially personal nature of their employment by a farmer. The fall in the numbers of women and children working on the land was also significant. The Gangs Act of 1867 (which introduced a licensing system in the employment of women and young people and forbade the employment of children under the age of eight) was of some importance in this respect, although the Education Acts had the greatest impact in the case of children.

In 1893 it was reported in Warwickshire that 'there has been now for the past ten or twenty years practically no agricultural work done by women, except to a slight extent in hay time and on allotments in harvest time. It is difficult to over-estimate the effect of this change on the condition of home life and the welfare of the children. Gleaning by women and children is still prevalent, but tends to decrease.'

Farmworkers, 1893

In these circumstances there was some evidence of a rise in the farm labourer's 'real wages'—i.e. in what he could really buy with the money that he received. Comparison with the wages of industrial workers is difficult because the custom of paying agricultural wages partly in kind continued: in the West Country employers sometimes supplied cider to their workers in accordance with ancient custom. It has been calculated, however, that the average wage of farm workers in Warwickshire was about 13s (65p) per week in 1870, 15s (75p) in 1892 and 17s (85p) in 1913, although the rise in the early years of the twentieth century was offset by a general rise in prices.

These, then were modest gains, but clearly in the right

direction. There were claims, too, that the farm worker benefited from the extension of education and from the gaining of the vote in the 1880's. For instance, in 1912 a writer suggested; 'labourers read, think, enquire. Their minds are awakening and curious for information.' The improvement of local government after the County Councils Act of 1888 also helped. Rural sanitary inspectors rooted out the worst abuses and campaigned in some areas at least for an improved water supply. The introduction of Old Age Pensions removed fear of one particular type of poverty.

In 1912 a contemporary observer sought to summarise the progress made since 1884:

'There can be no doubt of his (i.e. the farm labourer's) progress since 1884. Most men of this class are still poorly paid; many are precariously employed and poorly housed; among all, poverty is chronic, and although destitution is rare, the dread of it is seldom absent. But, speaking generally, labourers in 1912 are better paid, more regularly employed, better housed, better fed, better clothed. They are better educated and more sober. Their hours of labour are shorter. They are secure of a pension for themselves and their wives in their old age. . . . Their wives and children are no longer driven by necessity to labour in the fields.'

In 1914 it is possible to point to British agriculture as being in a generally depressed state, although the picture was not entirely black. It was to take two major wars to bring home to the nation the need to revive the prosperity of what earlier had been the country's major industry.

The Impact of the First World War

In 1914 Britain went to war with Germany. The struggle was to last for four years. It was a struggle in which the life of the whole nation had to be organised to ensure that the country survived. The effect of all this on the life of Britain was deep and lasting.

Perhaps the word 'organise' is of particular importance here. Unlike other nations of Europe, Britain in 1914 did not have a huge army based on conscription. She was thus faced with the problem of creating a vast citizen army in a short space of time.

At first this was to be a volunteer army, raised with the help of recruiting posters, public meetings and parades. The problems of clothing, feeding and training this army were, of course, very great. These problems were to be continuous. In 1916 conscription was introduced: ultimately a staggering 12·4 per cent of the population was in the armed forces.

The art of massive organisation was not learned easily. For a period some of the families of the men who rushed to join the army

Ladies' Fire Brigade, 1916

at the beginning of war were left virtually destitute. The rush of men to the colours left many industries dangerously short of highly-skilled craftsmen. The supply of ammunition was poor: in 1915 it was found that British field guns on the Western Front were rationed to four shells apiece per day.

Although some highly-skilled men were returned to industry, the war produced a great shortage of labour. Much of the work which had previously been the preserve of men was now done by women. In the four years of war about 1,500,000 women joined the labour force. Some of the jobs, such as those of coalmen, railway workers and colliery surface workers, were of a temporary nature. The women were to withdraw at the end of the war; but other work, for example in shops, offices and, to some extent transport, tended to remain in women's hands even after 1918.

The effect of all this on the status of women was to be profound. Not surprisingly, the vote was extended to women, although at first not on exactly equal terms with men, after the end of the Great War.

The war had a profound impact in other ways. To some extent, and in certain ways, it resulted in a narrowing of a gap between rich and poor. Taxation rose: it accounted for only 7·5 per cent of the national income in 1914, but a massive 18 per cent in 1919. Surtax was raised. A combination of death duties and a high death rate reduced the wealth of vast estates. On the other hand, it is well to remember that even in 1921 there were 1·3 million domestic servants in Britain.

To some extent there were changes in factory life on the home front. The needs of war accelerated the rate of industrial change: Britain experienced yet another 'industrial revolution' as more and more machine tools, some from the United States and Switzerland, were introduced. Wage rates for the semi-skilled machine operators rose as their numbers grew in British industry. A number of appalling accidents in munition factories drew attention to the need for improved safety regulations generally. The nation also came to realise the importance for industry of good welfare facilities: 867 works canteens were opened between 1915 and 1918. Medical centres, washrooms, sports clubs, even crèches were attached to factories. In 1916 the National Insurance Act of 1911 was extended to cover all workers.

At the same time there was an extension of a mass-production technique. Work study came more into its own: output bonus systems were pioneered. Attempts were made to apply the results of research more systematically to industrial processes.

The trade unions entered a new phase. The question of the employment of women and less-skilled men to take over the jobs of men who had gone into the armed forces produced tensions. In 1915 trade union leaders and the Government reached broad agreement on this dilution issue. For a period strikes were outlawed. Up to a point, the Government, by calling for the active co-operation of the trade unions, confirmed the importance of the unions in the national life. On the other hand, some workers felt that their leaders had not fought hard enough: this produced the 'shop stewards' movement' as men sought to put more power in the hands of trade union leaders who actually worked 'on the shop floor'.

Of course, many of the social services suffered in the war.

The building of schools slowed down. Hospital services were stretched to the point where schools and village halls had to be used, although the war led to advances in surgery and (in view of the large number of cases of 'shell shock') an increased interest in the treatment of nervous diseases.

House building also came to a virtual standstill during the war and the cost of houses soared. Indeed there was a general price rise: in 1919 the pound was worth only 9s 3d (47p) in terms of 1914 prices.

Demands on the police force were also great. High wages for civilian workers, and the determination of soldiers on leave to enjoy life whilst they could, tended to increase drunkenness, so that the Government had to step in with stricter licensing laws and the King himself set an example by giving up alcoholic drinks for the duration of the war. In London police problems were particularly severe, and it is interesting to note that more women were drafted in to help the police forces there.

An increasing interference by the Government in the life of the nation became apparent. For the first time responsibility was taken for seeing that the ordinary Englishman was well-fed. A Ministry of Food was set up; the Government bought and distributed food from Australia and New Zealand; in 1918 the

Distribution of sugar cards

rationing of meat, sugar, butter and eggs was introduced. At the same time an attempt was made to revive British agriculture. It will be remembered that in 1914, 40 per cent of meat on British tables came from abroad and that Britain imported 80 per cent of its grain supplies—facts that were very serious when, in 1917, German submarines set out to sink 600,000 tons of British shipping per month. In these circumstances British food production was increased by the ploughing up of rough pasture, the provision of several thousand tractors and the guaranteeing of prices for crops.

In other ways, too, the control of the Government in the country's life increased. Ministries of Pensions and Labour were set up. National problems were analysed with the help of carefully collected statistics. National factories were built (73 in 1915 alone): control of the railways and mines was established. Gradually the idea that the State had a part to play in improving life in 'a land fit for heroes' came to be accepted by an increasing number of people.

Documents

Improvements in Town Life, 1870–1914

A reminder of the wretched conditions which existed in the richest nation in the world.
Andrew Mearns, The Bitter Cry of Outcast London (*London, 1883*). *Quotation taken from the Leicester University Press 1970 edition, pp. 55, 58-59.*

Whilst we have been building our churches and solacing ourselves with our religion and dreaming that the millenium was coming, the poor have been growing poorer, the wretched more miserable, and the immoral more corrupt; the gulf has been daily widening which separates the lowest classes of the community from our churches and chapels, and from all decency and civilization. It is easy to bring an array of facts which seem to point to the opposite conclusion—to speak of the noble army of men and women who penetrate the vilest haunts, carrying with them the blessings of the gospel; of the encouraging reports published by Missions, Reformatories, Refuges, Temperance Societies; of Theatre Services, Midnight Meetings and Special Missions. But what does it all amount to? We are simply living in a fool's paradise if we suppose that all these agencies combined are doing a thousandth part of what needs to be done, a hundredth part of what *could* be done by the Church of Christ. We must face the facts; and these compel the conviction that THIS TERRIBLE FLOOD OF SIN AND MISERY IS GAINING UPON US. It is rising every day. This statement is made as the result of a long, patient and sober inquiry, undertaken for the purpose of discovering the actual state of the case and the remedial action most likely to be effective. Convinced that it is high time some combined and organised effort was made by all denominations of Christians, though not for denominational purposes, the London Congregational Union have determined to open in several of the lowest and most needy districts of the metropolis, suitable Mission Halls, as a base of operations for evangelistic work. They have accordingly made this diligent search, and some of the results are set forth in the following pages, in the hope that all who have the power may be stimulated to help the Union in the great and difficult enterprise which they have undertaken.

Two cautions it is important to bear in mind. First, the information given *does not refer to selected cases*. It simply reveals a state of things which is found in house after house, court after court, street after street. Secondly, there *has been absolutely no exaggeration*. It is a plain recital of plain facts. Indeed, no respectable printer would print, and certainly no decent family would admit even the driest statement of the horrors and infamies discovered in one brief visitation from house to house. *So far from making the worst of our facts for the purpose of appealing to emotion, we have been compelled to tone down everything, and wholly to omit what most needs to be known, or the ears and eyes of our readers would have been insufferably outraged.* Yet even this qualified narration must be to every Christian heart a loud and bitter cry, appealing for the help which it is the supreme mission of the Church to supply. It should be further stated that our investigations were made in the summer. The condition of the poor during the winter months must be very much worse. . . .

Think of

THE CONDITION IN WHICH THEY LIVE.

We do not say the condition of their homes, for how can those places be called homes, compared with which the lair of a wild beast would be a comfortable and healthy spot? Few who will read these pages have any conception of what these pestilential human rookeries are, where tens of thousands are crowded together amidst horrors which call to mind what we have heard of the middle passage of the slave ship. To get into them you have to penetrate courts reeking with poisonous and malodorous gases arising from the accumulations of sewage and refuse scattered in all directions and often flowing beneath your feet; courts, many of them which the sun never penetrates, which are never visited by a breath of fresh air, and which rarely know the virtues of a drop of cleansing water. You have to ascend rotten staircases, which threaten to give way beneath every step, and which, in some cases, have already broken down, leaving gaps that imperil the limbs and lives of the unwary. You have to grope your way along dark and filthy passages swarming with vermin. Then, if you are not driven back by the intolerable stench, you may gain admittance to the dens in which these thousands of beings who belong, as much as you, to the race for whom Christ died, herd together. Have you pitied the poor creatures who sleep under railway arches, in carts or casks, or under any shelter which they can find in the open air? You will see that they are to be envied in comparison with those whose lot it is to seek refuge here. Eight feet square—that is about the average size of very many of these rooms. Walls and ceilings are black with the accretions of filth which have gathered upon them in the boards overhead; it is running down the walls; it is everywhere. What goes by the name of a window is half of it stuffed with rags or covered by boards to keep out wind and rain; the rest is so begrimed and obscured that scarcely can light enter or anything be seen outside. Should you have ascended to the attic, where at least some approach to fresh air might be expected to enter from open or broken window, you look out upon the roofs and ledges of lower tenements, and discover that the sickly air which finds its way into the room has to pass over the putrefying carcases of dead cats or birds, or viler abominations still. The buildings are in such miserable repair as to suggest the thought that if the wind could only reach them they would soon be toppling about the heads of their occupants. As to furniture—you may perchance discover a broken chair, the tottering relics of an old bedstead, or the mere fragment of a table; but more commonly you will find rude substitutes for these things in the shape of rough boards resting upon bricks, an old hamper or box turned upside down, or more frequently still, nothing but rubbish and rags.

The Nation's Health, 1870–1914

A contemporary describes a typical pre-1914 middle class diet and contrasts it with that of a typical labourer.
Quoted in A. Marwick, The Deluge (London, 1965), pp. 196–7.

The middle-class menu ran [in pre-war England]:

FRIDAY. *Breakfast:* fish cakes, sardines, fried bacon, bread, butter, marmalade, tea, coffee. *Dinner:* rabbits, potatoes, gooseberry tart, rice pudding, cream, sugar. *Tea:* bread, butter, jam, cakes, tea. *Supper:* cheese, biscuits, bread, butter, cakes, cocoa.

SATURDAY. *Breakfast:* fish, sardines, fried bacon, bread, butter, marmalade, tea, coffee. *Dinner:* beefsteak, potatoes, cauliflower, queen of puddings, rice pudding, cream. *Tea:* bread, butter, marmalade, cakes, tea. *Supper:* cheese, biscuits, bread, butter, cakes, cocoa, milk, coffee.

SUNDAY. *Breakfast:* bacon, poached eggs, bread, butter, marmalade, tea, coffee. *Dinner:* roast beef, Yorkshire pudding, roast potatoes, rice pudding, gooseberry tart, cream, sugar. *Tea:* bread, butter, jam, cakes, tea. *Supper:* cheese, biscuits, bread, butter, cake, cocoa, milk.

MONDAY. *Breakfast:* bacon, sardines, bread, butter, marmalade, tea, coffee. *Dinner:* cold beef, salad, potatoes, sponge cake, custard pudding, rice. *Tea:* bread, butter, cakes, marmalade, tea. *Supper:* eggs, biscuits, bread, butter, cakes, cocoa, milk.

TUESDAY. *Breakfast:* fried bacon, poached eggs, bread, butter, marmalade, tea, coffee. *Dinner:* cold beef, salad, hashed beef, potatoes, stewed fruit, rice pudding. *Tea:* bread, butter, cakes, marmalade, tea. *Supper:* cheese, biscuits, bread, butter, cakes, cocoa, coffee, milk.

WEDNESDAY. *Breakfast:* fried bacon, sardines, bread, butter, marmalade, tea, coffee. *Dinner:* roast mutton, jelly, potatoes, cabbage, gooseberry tart, pancakes. *Tea:* bread, butter, cakes, jam, marmalade, tea. *Supper:* cheese, biscuits, bread, butter, cakes, cocoa, milk.

THURSDAY. *Breakfast:* chicken and tongue mould, bread, butter, marmalade, tea, coffee. *Dinner:* cold mutton, potatoes, salad, curry, rice pudding, stewed fruit. *Tea:* bread, butter, cakes, jam, marmalade, tea. *Supper:* cheese, biscuits, bread, butter, cakes, cocoa, milk.

The labourer's pre-war menu read as follows:

FRIDAY. *Breakfast:* bread, cheese, tea. *Dinner:* potatoes, bread, tea. *Tea:* bread, butter, tea.

SATURDAY. *Breakfast:* 'dip', bread, butter, tea. *Dinner:* sausages, bread. *Tea:* bread, cocoa, jam, tea.

SUNDAY. *Breakfast:* bacon, bread, toast, tea. *Dinner:* meat, potatoes, Yorkshire pudding. *Tea:* bread, pie, tea cakes, tea.

MONDAY. *Breakfast:* bacon, bread, tea. *Dinner:* bacon, bread, tea. *Tea:* bacon, bread, tea.

TUESDAY. *Breakfast:* bread, meat, tea. *Dinner:* meat, bread, tea. *Tea:* meat, bread, tea.
WEDNESDAY. *Breakfast:* bacon, bread, tea. *Dinner:* meat, bread, tea. *Tea:* eggs, 'dip', bread, tea.
THURSDAY. *Breakfast:* bread, butter, tea. *Dinner:* meat, bread, 'dip', tea. *Tea:* meat, bread, butter, tea.

Social Security, 1870–1914

Lloyd George explains his support of the 1911 National Insurance Act, one of the major pre-war social reforms.
Quoted in W. H. B. *Court* British Economic History, 1870–1914. Commentary and Documents (*Cambridge, 1965*), *pp. 415–17.*

Now comes the question, which leads up to the decision of the Government to take action. What is the explanation that only a portion of the working-classes have made provision against sickness and against unemployment? Is it they consider it not necessary? Quite the reverse, as I shall prove by figures. In fact, those who stand most in need of it make up the bulk of the uninsured. Why? Because very few can afford to pay the premiums, and pay them continuously, which enable a man to provide against those three contingencies. As a matter of fact, you could not provide against all those three contingencies anything which would be worth a workman's while, without paying at any rate 1s. 6d. or 2s. per week at the very lowest. There are a multitude of the working classes who cannot spare that, and ought not to be asked to spare it, because it involves the deprivation of children of the necessaries of life. Therefore they are compelled to elect, and the vast majority choose to insure against death alone. Those who can afford to take up two policies insure against death and sickness, and those who can afford to take up all three insure against death, sickness and unemployment, but only in that order. What are the explanations why they do not insure against all three? The first is that their wages are too low. I am talking now about the uninsured portion. The wages are too low to enable them to insure against all three without some assistance. The second difficulty, and it is the greatest of all, is that during a period of sickness or unemployment, when they are earning nothing, they cannot keep up the premiums. They may be able to do it for a fortnight or three weeks, but when times of very bad trade come, when a man is out of work for weeks and weeks at a time, arrears run up with the friendly societies, and when the man gets work, it may be at the end of two or three months, those are not the first arrears which have to be met. There are arrears of rent, arrears of the grocery bill, and arrears for the necessaries of life. At any rate he cannot consider his friendly society only. The result is that a very considerable number of workmen find themselves quite unable to keep up the premiums when they have a family to look after.

Undoubtedly there is another reason. It is no use shirking the fact that a proportion of workmen with good wages spend them in other ways, and therefore have nothing to spare with which to pay premiums to friendly societies. It has come to my notice, in many of these cases, that the women of the family make most heroic efforts to keep up the premiums to the friendly societies, and the officers of friendly societies, whom I have seen, have amazed me by telling the proportion of premiums of this kind paid by women out of the very wretched allowance given them to keep the household together. I think it is well we should look all the facts in the face before we come to consider the remedy. What does it mean in the way of lapses? I have inquired of friendly societies, and, as near as I can get at it, there are 250,000 lapses in a year. That is a very considerable proportion of the 6,000,000 policies. The expectation of life at twenty is, I think, a little over forty years, and it means that in twenty years' time there are 5,000,000 lapses; that is, people who supported and joined friendly societies, and who have gone on paying the premiums for weeks, months, and even years, struggling along, at last, when a very bad time of unemployment comes, drop out and the premium lapses. It runs to millions in the course of a generation. What does it mean? It means that the vast majority of the working men of this country at one time or other have been members of friendly societies, have felt the need for provision of this kind and it is only because they have been driven, sometimes by their own habits, but in the majority of cases by circumstances over which they have no control—to abandon their policies. That is the reason why, at the present moment, not one half of the workmen of this country have made any provision for sickness, and not one-tenth for unemployment. I think it necessary to state these facts in order to show that there is a real need for some system which would aid the workmen over these difficulties. I do not think there is any better method, or one more practicable at the present moment, than a system of national insurance which would invoke the aid of the State and the aid of the employer to enable the workman to get over all these difficulties and make provision for himself for sickness, and, as far as the most precarious trades are concerned, against unemployment.

The Middle Classes, 1870–1914

Mrs. Beeton's guide for the middle and upper class housewife on the engagement and management of domestic servants.
Isabella Beaton, Book of Household Management (*London 1907 ed.*) *pp. 1761–2.*

Masters and Mistresses

It is said that good masters and mistresses make good servants, and this to a great extent is true. There are certainly some men and women whom it would be impossible to train into good servants, but the conduct of both master and mistress is seldom without its effect upon these dependents. The sensible master and the kind mistress know, that if servants depend on them for their means of living, in their turn they are dependent on their servants for very many of the comforts of life; and that using a proper amount of care in choosing servants, treating them like reasonable beings and making slight excuses for the shortcomings of human nature, they will be tolerably well served, and surround themselves with attached domestics.

Women servants are specially likely to be influenced by their mistress's treatment of them. In many cases mistresses do not give their servants the help which it is their duty to afford. A timely hint, or even a few words of quiet reproof, may be lacking when needed, and still more so the kind words and the deserved praise for work well and carefully done. It is a fact that we must take some trouble with our servants. There is no necessity for a mistress to be continually fussing round and superintending her servants' work, but she must first make sure that they do it thoroughly and well. Also she must take time and pains to show her domestics how she likes the work done.

A strict mistress is not necessarily a harsh one, and for the sake of others as well as herself she should insist upon the daily duties of each servant being faithfully and punctually performed. Every mistress should know for herself how long it takes for each household task, and it is then easy to see whether or no time has been wasted.

Work hurried is pretty nearly sure to be work ill done; and it is a fact that cannot be too firmly impressed upon all, that time must be proportionate to labour, and that a fair amount of rest should be regular and certain. In large households with a full staff of servants it is comparatively easy to have order, regularity and comfort, but when there are but few, or it may be only one woman servant, then the mistress has much to think of and to do. There are not only so many ways in which we may assist our servants, there are twice as many in which we can save them labour, and in which we can show them how to save themselves.

They for their own part having chosen their own way of earning their livelihood should be only too ready and willing to learn to rise in an honourable calling such as service is, and where their comfort and welfare is made the care of the mistress, it should surely be their pleasure as well as their duty to serve her to the best of their ability. . . .

The treatment of servants is of the greatest importance to both mistress and domestics. If the latter perceive that their mistress's conduct is regulated by high and correct principles, they will not fail to respect her; and if a real desire is shown to promote their comfort, while at the same time a steady performance of their duty is exacted, then well-principled servants will be anxious to earn approval, and their respect will not be unmingled with affection.

A lady should never allow herself to forget the importance of watching over the moral and physical welfare of those beneath her roof. Without seeming unduly inquisitive, she can always learn something of their acquaintances and holiday occupation, and should, when necessary, warn them against the dangers and evils of bad company. An hour should be fixed, usually 10 or 9 p.m., after which no servant should be allowed to stay out. To permit breaches of this rule, without having good and explicit reasons furnished, is very far from being a kindness to the servant concerned. The moral responsibility for evil that may result rests largely on the employer who permits late hours. Especial care is needed with young girls. They should be given opportunities for welcoming respectable friends at their employer's house, and not be forced by absence of such provision for their comfort to spend their spare time out of doors, often in driving rain, possibly in bad company. . . .

Number of servants suited to different incomes.—The following is a rough scale of servants suited to various incomes. It is, however, impossible to give any general rule in these matters. Whether in a household of moderate means such as our scales deal with, a man-servant is required, will depend upon whether the house is situated in town or country, and if the possession of horses or a garden renders his services imperative. One should not forget that when heavy expenses such as those of education have to be incurred for a family, this outlay must be carefully allowed for, before committing oneself in other directions. Similarly, where two servants are kept, and a nurse is required for young children, it will probably be deemed wise to dispense with the services of the house-maid, and arrange for the nurse to give some help to the cook.

When one is considering if an extra servant is necessary or not, it is well to remember that assistance may sometimes be profitably arranged by engaging a lad for two or three hours a day to do such rough work as cleaning boots and shoes, working in the garden, etc.; and, when uncertain whether to engage a gardener, one should not forget that a man not coming more than four days a week does not render an employer liable to the duty on man-servants.

About £1,000 a year. Cook, housemaid, and perhaps a man-servant.
From £750 to £500 a year. Cook, housemaid.
About £300 a year. General servant.
About £200 a year. Young girl for rough work.

The Land, 1870–1914

An 1884–5 report on working class housing describes the farm labourer's cottage. Rural progress was unevenly felt.
Quoted in E. Royston Pike, Human Documents of the Age of the Forsytes (*London, 1969*), *pp. 194–6.*

At the conclusion of their inquiry into working class dwellings in urban centres of population Your Majesty's Commissioners commenced their rural investigation by first calling a number of persons who represented the interests of the agricultural labourers in different counties. . . .

Mr Selby, an agent of the Agricultural Labourers' Union, and formerly a labourer himself, testified to the condition of certain parts of Wiltshire, to which he had paid special attention. In one village he described several cottages in which the structural defects were considerable. The bedrooms in one case were not high enough to stand up in, and in another case two small bedrooms, each of which was entirely filled by the bed, were occupied by a man and his wife and seven children, from 16 years of age downwards. In another there was a case of a widow and her family of six, the eldest son being 25, sleeping in one bedroom. At a third, a labourer and his daughter, with her husband and six children, all slept in one bedroom, not more than 14 feet square, the sloping roof at the highest point being about 7 feet from the ground; but in that case there appeared to be a downstairs room not used for sleeping purposes.

In the rural districts there is less plea for absolute necessity for overcrowding in sleeping rooms than in the metropolis, that is to say, the single room system, as it is found in the metropolis, has no existence in agricultural villages. Single room cottages—those containing only one room for all purposes—are found in rare cases; as a rule, the most miserably housed families in the rural districts have another room in addition to the sleeping chamber, and it is from habit or from the nature of the room that they do not utilize the living apartment for the purposes of sleeping. Two roomed houses in some localities in this and in other counties are very common, and it is in them that the worst overcrowding exists. The structural and sanitary condition of some of the cottages of Wiltshire was described to be very bad. At another village they were found to be falling to pieces from neglect; in some cases the bare thatch being visible upstairs and letting in the rain.

Mr Samuel Pike, another agent of the Union, gave evidence as to Dorset and parts of the adjacent counties. He described the sanitary condition of cottages as very defective; some have no stairs but a ladder by which to walk up to the upper rooms, and no stone or board on the floors, only the earth, or perhaps worn-away concrete. In this district Mr Pike said that the cottages of the labourers chiefly contained one small room downstairs and two upstairs, and that there was under these conditions overcrowding of the kind described. There was a case of 11 persons, two parents and nine children, including a boy of 19 and a girl of 15, occupying two small rooms. Similar evidence was given from the neighbouring county of Somerset.

Mr Alfred Simmons, the secretary of the Kent and Sussex Labourers' Union, spoke of the improvement that had taken place in some portions of his district in the cottage accommodation, but described the sanitary conditions as very bad indeed.

Mr George Ball, the agent of the Labourers' Union in Essex, said that generally speaking the cottage accommodation in the rural districts of that county was, to quote his words, 'very sad indeed', at one village visited by him one bedroom was the rule. In another, which he described as the worst village in Essex [Steeple Brompstead], he found the cottages both badly constructed and in bad repair, few of them having rooms more than 6 or 7 feet high, and there were numerous instances of overcrowding.

The Rev C. W. Stubbs described the condition of the labourers' cottages in certain 'open' [i.e. not all owned by one landlord] villages in Buckinghamshire. His late parish of Granborough contained about 50 cottages; of these only one had more than two bedrooms, and 17 had only one bedroom, and he described the 'wattle and dab' huts in which the poor are most frequently housed in that county. These have usually a lean-to at the end of the cottage in which the people store their things, and in one corner of which there is an open privy draining into the nearest ditch.

In contrast to the foregoing may be cited instances in which great improvements have been carried out, with the result of the cottagers being housed in comfort and under sanitary conditions ... but while many landowners have shown considerable interest in the work of the better housing of their poorest tenants, it cannot be denied that there are cases in which the condition described can be traced to the neglect of the freeholder.

In Wiltshire a very common rent seems to be about 1s. a week, while the averages of wages are put at from 9s. to 13s. a week. The wages of a shepherd in the same county, who earns 16s. a week all the year round, and has besides a cottage and garden, may be considered an exceptional instance. Shepherds, moreover, like carters and certain other servants, have to work for very long hours and also on Sundays. In Dorsetshire there was said to be no uniform rate. In one district where the wages are about 11s. the rent of small cottages was said to be about 7s. a month, that is to say, 1s. 9d. a week. In Essex the agent to the Labourers' Union stated that the wages of ordinary farm labourers average 11s. a week, while the rent of cottages he computes at about 1s. 8d. a week ...

The occupation of a cottage is sometimes considered as part of a man's weekly wages. This is the case where cottages are let with the farms and sublet by the farmers. This, in the opinion of the men themselves, is said to be one of the greatest grievances that they have to suffer from. They are engaged at so much a week and the cottage, and the hardship is stated to be that as it is reckoned part of their wages they are liable to be, and sometimes are, turned out at a week's notice. There is evidence from different parts of England that there is more dissatisfaction among the labourers with regard to this part of the cottage question than about anything else; the insecurity of the tenure is felt more severely even than the misery of the accommodation.

War 1914–18

The adaptation of women to a wartime situation as reported in the Daily Mail, *14th September 1915 and 17th April 1916.*

NEW GIRTON GIRLS.

FROM THE HOCKEY STICK TO THE HOE.

Eight of the first squad of fifteen East Anglian girls trained at the Cambridge University School of Agriculture for educated women have already obtained appointments. The members of the squad were selected for their physical fitness; many of them are hockey players, a few of them good horsewomen.

They are lodged at Girton College. They have been put to all sorts of work on the University Farm and the plant-breeding farm—digging, hoeing, drilling, guiding the cultivator, carting, tending the horses and stock, and milking. As an experiment three of them have received instruction in thatching and show promise, though the experiment is not yet a definite success. Those who work horses are up at 5.30 a.m.; those who milk start at six. The girls get on well with the horses, but were rather timid at first of the cows.

As regards clothing, they are practically all in favour of the skirt—which must be short—with breeches, gaiters, and stout boots—not boys' boots but boots of the kind girls wear to play hockey or to go out walking in.

DINING-OUT GIRLS.

A WAR-WORK INNOVATION.

The war-time business girl is to be seen any night dining out alone or with a friend in the moderate-priced restaurants in London. Formerly she would never have had her evening meal in town unless in the company of a man friend. But now with money and without men she is more and more beginning to dine out.

Most often they are in couples, though not infrequently one sees merry groups of three or four. After a modest dinner cigarettes follow, and then there is talk of typing, "governors," theatres, and dress. Very often girls look in for only a cup of coffee, with, again, the customary cigarette.

With flashing mirrors and gleaming lights, music at intervals, and the constantly changing company there is a mingling of cheapness, comfort, and mild diversion which is evidently very attractive. It is the beginning of the evolution of the business girl as a woman of the world.

Part II

Britain 1918–1970
by B. J. Elliott

(i) BRITISH SOCIETY 1918–1939

The Industrial Worker

By 1914 Britain had made much less progress in the advanced industries—chemicals, electricals, motors and machine tools—than her main competitors, the U.S.A. and Germany. Britain still relied on her older industries such as coal, cotton, ships and railway materials. The sale of these goods paid for the food, drink, timber, iron-ore and other raw materials which 40 million Britons needed.

After the First World War Britain found it difficult to sell her cotton, coal and heavy iron and steel goods to other countries. Export sales fell and hundreds of thousands of men and women, living in Scotland, South Wales, Lancashire and North East England, lost their jobs. Whilst these industries suffered, new ones were growing up. The most important were electricals, motor-cars, aircraft, chemicals and artificial fibres (silk and rayon). The factories which made these goods used electricity instead of steam engines for power and so did not need to be built near the coalfields. They were set up in the Midlands and around London and so could not offer jobs to Scots, Welshmen and Tynesiders. There was a great deal of work in the building trades in the 1930's but again far away from the 'distressed areas'.

National Hunger March, 1932

 The cotton industry based in Lancashire made its profit by exporting about 70 per cent of its production. After 1914 India and Japan began to make large amounts of cotton goods more cheaply and British exports fell heavily. Lancashire had hundreds of small high-cost firms which could not compete. Many went bankrupt, others were swallowed up into larger groups. Between 1930–8 over 30 per cent (170,000) of cotton workers lost their jobs and the amount of machinery was reduced by one-third.

 The shipbuilding industry had expanded during the war to supply new warships and replacements for freighters sunk by torpedoes. By 1920 there were too many ships in the world for the amount of trade and too many shipyards which were not needed. The great powers—U.S.A., Britain, Japan, France and Italy—were discussing how to cut down on naval building. Unemployment amongst shipyard workers in such centres as Glasgow, Sunderland, Belfast and Jarrow was amongst the highest of all trades. By 1933 the total of new tonnage launched was only seven per cent of that of 1913. When Palmers shipyard in Jarrow stopped work in 1932 73 per cent of the town became unemployed. The government encouraged the closure of many yards such as Palmers, but it also lent money to ship-owners to scrap old vessels and order new ones. On Clydeside work on the *Queen Mary* and *Queen Elizabeth* helped to get many men back to work.

 The iron and steel industry was seriously affected by the

slump in shipbuilding and the end of railway-building in Britain, the U.S.A., Europe and many other parts of the world. In 1931 almost half the nation's steelworkers were out of work. One reason was that, as in shipbuilding, many works had been greatly expanded during the First World War. Others in Scotland and Cumberland were outdated and inefficient. These works were forced to close but new works at Corby, Scunthorpe and Ebbw Vale were opened and the steel industry recovered well. Production, which had fallen to 5·2 million tonnes in 1931, rose to a record 13·7 million tonnes in 1937. One reason for this was that Britain was rebuilding her armed forces to meet the possibility of war with Germany, Italy or Japan.

Overshadowing all others in its difficulties and distress was the coal industry. By 1920 this industry employed 1·226 million men producing 226 million tonnes of coal. The prosperity of the British mines also rested upon large exports. At first there was no problem. The coal mines of France and Belgium had been damaged in the war and in Germany (1922) and the U.S.A. (1923) there were great strikes. By 1925, however, the British industry was in difficulties. German and Polish coal exports were capturing British markets. Many of Britain's mines especially in Scotland, Durham and South Wales were old and exhausted. There was little money available to sink new mines except in the East Midlands. Furthermore, the world did not need so much coal. Ships were changing to oil-fired engines and on land motor vehicles were beginning to capture traffic from steam railways. Engineers were learning how to extract more energy from the same amount of fuel. Then in March 1925 Britain went back on to the 'gold standard'. This meant that a foreign buyer had to pay $4.85 for one pound's worth of British goods or coal. This was about ten per cent more than the pound was really worth and coal exports fell further.

Coal production fell to 208 million tonnes in 1932-3, about 30 per cent less than the all-time record of 1913. The coal owners began to dismiss workers or offer only part-time work. Of the 1·226 million in 1920 only about 800,000 were still registered miners by the mid-1930's. In parts of the North East and South Wales whole villages became unemployed when the local pits closed. There was no other work available for either men or women unless they moved. Many hundreds of thousands moved from South Wales, Scotland and the North East. Some went to Commonwealth countries but by 1930 Australia, Canada and other such countries had their own serious economic problems. Many emigrants returned to Britain.

The most popular places in Britain for finding new jobs were London and the South East, the West Midlands where the car industry was growing up and the East Midlands coalfield. Those who stayed behind in the 'old' coalfields existed on Unemployment Insurance benefits, sometimes for several years. Eventually these benefits stopped and the workless had to turn to the Poor Law Guardians for 'relief' payments. For the older men there was no prospect of work at all until the Second World War.

Despite the fact that unemployment was the most serious threat facing workers between 1919 and 1940, the new growing industries of the South East and the Midlands offered a very different kind of working life. The establishment of new factories far from the coalfields was the result of the growth of one of these industries—electricity supply. The Central Electricity Board set up a national 'grid' of transmission cables which linked up nearly 150 power stations across the country. Many thousands of men were employed providing the electricity supply until by 1938 almost nine million houses, offices and factories were provided for. The supply of electricity made it possible for people to buy electric gramophones, radios, irons, vacuum cleaners and, for a lucky few, washing machines and refrigerators.

Of equal importance in providing work were the motor vehicle and aircraft industries.

By 1938 the total number employed in the electrical and motor industries equalled that in coal mining. The motor industry developed greatly during the war and was also able to learn American mass-production techniques. Austin and Morris in the Midlands and Ford at Dagenham were the largest producers concentrating on the cheap family car. By 1937 annual production topped 500,000 cars; in addition many thousands of motor-cycles, lorries and buses were manufactured. By streamlining production methods and aiming at a large market the car-makers were able to bring prices down by 50 per cent between 1924 and 1936. Whilst some luxury cars were handbuilt, the cheaper ones came down production lines which meant the work was lighter, but repetitive and boring.

Aircraft building depended upon the Royal Air Force for its main orders because civil aviation was developing only slowly. Some 30,000 men and women earned their living in this industry which centred on the London area, Bristol and Derby.

The chemical industry, like aircraft, motors, and electricals, demanded highly educated scientific research teams and large quantities of capital to build up new and expensive processes. By 1939 four firms controlled the major sectors of chemicals. Courtaulds and British Celanese dominated the manufacture of man-made fibres such as rayon. Imperial Chemical Industries, a merger of four firms in 1926, produced almost all heavy and light chemicals in Britain. Plate-glass manufacture was in the hands of Pilkingtons of St. Helens.

British industry between the two World Wars went through the painful process of trying to move away from the massive, simple production of the nineteenth century such as coal and cotton. New scientific industries began to grow, but this change caused suffering and difficulties. It left hundreds of thousands of men and women stranded in 'distressed areas' without work, in towns and villages which themselves were as old and worked-out as the industries which had collapsed.

Town Life

Between 1920 and 1938 the total population of Britain rose by 2·7 million, with the biggest increases taking place in the South East, the Midlands and the West Riding of Yorkshire. Most of this increased population lived in the larger cities and towns. London grew from 7·48 to 8·20 million. Birmingham increased by 130,000 to 1·05 million between the same years. Some towns, particularly Birmingham and Sheffield, had also grown considerably during the war years as workers poured into the munitions factories.

House-building, however, had almost come to a stop during the war years because there were neither men, materials nor money to spare. Thus Birmingham which had 50,000 houses classed as 'unfit for human habitation' in 1913 had to find accommodation for 79,000 more people between 1911 and 1921. Sheffield's population rose by 63,000 between these two years yet only 1,000 more houses were added during the war. Most other big cities had serious problems. Leeds had 70,000 back-to-backs; Manchester had 30,000 condemned as 'unfit'. Overcrowding was particularly serious. The worst areas in order were Stepney (London), the Gorbals (Glasgow), Netherfield (Liverpool), Westgate (Newcastle) and Medlock (Manchester), where between 130 and 240 persons per acre (0·4 hectares) were to be found. These were the central areas of older industrial cities where the three-roomed house was most common.

Lloyd George, the wartime Prime Minister, had promised 'homes fit for heroes'. In the past workers had been unable to rent decent houses because of low wages. Rent controls came in during the war and by 1919 it was obvious that if homes were to be provided for the heroes the government would have to help with the cost of building. During the first few years of peace three important acts were passed to try to improve the housing situation. These were the Addison Act (1919), the Chamberlain Act (1923) and the Wheatley Act (1924). As a result some 750,000 new houses were built but most were for people earning comfortable, if not high, wages.

Houses of the nineteen-thirties

This activity in the 1920's increased in the 1930's to create vast new suburbs around London, Birmingham and the other great cities of Britain. At Becontree in Essex the London County Council began in 1921 to build a new housing estate. By 1932 it had a population of 100,000. The Kingstanding estate in Birmingham housed 30,000.

Families from the desperately overcrowded central wards were rehoused mainly in the 'outer ring' suburbs. Between 1920–38 Birmingham's 'outer ring' increased its population by 91 per cent as a result of the 84,000 new houses, whilst the central and 'middle' ring areas each fell by about 23 per cent.

These new houses were a great improvement on the Victorian back-to-backs and Edwardian terraces. Most were semi-detached with two or three bedrooms, kitchen, parlour, bathroom, inside lavatory, electricity and gas. However, the estates were often bleak and isolated. Often several years passed before shops, pubs, cinemas, libraries and churches were all established. Instead of being able to walk to work, the new tenants had to pay bus-fares as well as higher rents. In the older areas few rents were more than 10s (50p) per week. In the new estates most were *above* that figure.

Very few slums were demolished in the 1920's because of the continued shortage of cheaply rented accommodation. In 1930 the second Labour government passed an act to begin the attack on slums. It was planned to demolish 266,000 slums and rehouse $1\frac{1}{4}$ million persons. Much was achieved. The L.C.C. built tower blocks of flats at Southwark, Wandsworth, St. Pancras and elsewhere. Bristol built 10,000 houses in the 1930's; the largest estates were at Knowle—Bedminster. Sheffield laid out new housing high above the city at Wybourn, Manor and Arbourthorne. Manchester began to work on a garden suburb at Wythenshawe and Glasgow at Pollok.

By 1939 more than 4 million houses had been built since the First World War of which more than 1·3 million were 'council' houses. There was probably a surplus of housing for people earning reasonable wages. For the million or so unemployed, the pensioners and those on low wages, the nineteenth century slums were still 'home'. Overcrowding was still a serious problem in Newcastle, Glasgow, Liverpool and Inner London.

The creation of new suburbs meant an extension of public transport, unless the tenants were expected to walk to work and to the central shopping areas. Only around London were new railways considered, because elsewhere the distances involved were usually less than 8 km.

Even in London these were merely extensions of existing lines such as to Edgware (1924), Morden (1926), Upminster (1932) and Cockfosters (1933). In an effort to make services faster and less costly, electrification was introduced in a number of commuter services, such as Altrincham–Manchester (1931) and London–Brighton (1933).

If railways were not the answer then neither were tramways. The big cities relied heavily upon tramcars to serve the central areas and the older suburbs but there were few extensions built after 1919. Some smaller towns scrapped tramways completely in favour of the

The mass-produced car

trolley bus. Amongst these were Doncaster, Ipswich, Lancaster and Worcester. Birmingham with 77 miles (124 km) of tram-route in 1926 could not scrap the lot but by 1937 it had given up 12 miles (19 km) whilst its bus routes rose from 65 to 153 miles (105 to 246 km). Sheffield did not allow buses to compete over the tram-route but between 1925–35 the number of routes (to villages and new estates) rose from 20 to 55 and the number of passengers from 1 million per year to 3·7 million.

   An even more common sight on the roads of Britain was the family car. By 1930 over a million were licensed, a figure which more than doubled by 1939. Traffic problems in the cities became increasingly serious. Traffic lights began to appear after 1929. One-way systems began in Birmingham and the 30-mile (48 km) speed limit and driving tests were introduced in 1934. Between the towns and villages were roads neglected for almost 100 years. These were tarmaced over and given numbers such as A10 but few completely new roads were built. There were no motorways built as in Germany and the U.S.A.

   Within the towns, if one could ignore the growing noise of

traffic, there were many new attractions. There were 4,000 cinema houses by the late 1920's with seats as cheap as 1p in some areas. There were inexpensive cafés. For the wealthy there were nightclubs in the larger cities. Many new shops were built both in the central areas and the new suburbs. Chain stores, such as Boots and Marks and Spencers, opened in many towns. The Co-operative Societies also spread to new areas, particularly in the Midlands and South East.

Public houses were less popular than before 1914, partly because there were other entertainments, partly because of unemployment. Perhaps the greatest change in the appearance of the towns came after dark when electric lighting both in the streets and in shop windows gave an air of brightness and gaiety which many people did not feel.

Education

The education service inevitably suffered during the First World War. Spending was reduced and no new schools or important repair works were possible. Thousands of male teachers left the classrooms for the trenches and overcrowded classes increased. Older children in elementary schools left early to take up paid work. This was very necessary in large families when the father had been called up.

If homes were to be provided for heroes after the war, it was also felt that schools should be provided fit for the sons and daughters of heroes. As early as 1915 a committee was set up to look into the provision of education after the war. In 1917 it reported, with the main suggestion that local authorities should be compelled to provide, and 14–18 year olds compelled to attend, day continuation classes (part-time education).

As the war drew to an end Parliament passed a major Education Act. It was the work of H. A. L. Fisher, President of the Board of Education from 1916–22. The 1918 'Fisher Act' included the setting up of day continuation classes. It also gave local authorities more powers, including the right to raise the school-leaving age to 15. Most importantly, it ended the 'half-time' system by which 13 and 14 year olds spent either the morning or afternoon in the factory or mill and the other half of the day in school. Children aged 12–14

A wireless lesson

were limited to two hours' paid work daily but excluded from mines, factories or street trading. It also ended fee-paying in elementary schools and allowed local authorities to give grants to secondary school pupils in need. The government share of the cost was also increased, so that a new pay scale for teachers could be worked out.

As in the case of housing, these fine new ideas had to be practically forgotten. By 1921 Britain was in economic difficulties and over a million were unemployed. Government spending was cut and education suffered as much as anything. Day classes for 14–18 year olds were scrapped, teachers were obliged to pay five per cent of their salaries towards their pensions, and spending on buildings, books and scholarships all suffered. For the remainder of this period up to 1939 most of the plans, such as raising the leaving age to 15, suffered from the need to cut back on national spending. Nevertheless, plans did appear which were generally regarded as being very good ideas for the future educational systems of Britain.

By far the most important of these plans were the reports of the Hadow Committee on the *Education of the Adolescent* (1926), *The Primary School* (1931) and *Infant and Nursery Schools* (1933). The 1926 report called for the ending of all-age schools, 5–14 years, to be replaced by primary education (5–11 years) and secondary education at eleven-plus in either 'grammar' or 'modern' schools. It was also suggested that the school-leaving age be raised to 15 in 1931. This would have required 350,000 extra school places and 12,000 more teachers. In 1930–1 the world economic crisis rapidly developed and Britain had to allow the devaluation of the pound. Naturally the government had no intention of spending a much greater sum on education at a time like this. Indeed almost all school building halted between 1931–6 and there was considerable unemployment amongst teachers.

The Hadow Reports on primary schools and infant and nursery schools were excellent documents. They explained in detail how and why young children learnt and the activities which were best suited to them. As a result primary school children slowly began to spend less time copying, memorising and chanting aloud. Individual project work, drama, play-learning, fieldwork and other activities became more a part of school life. There were other exciting developments. Wireless lessons broadcast by the B.B.C. began in 1924 and by 1939 several thousand schools were 'listening in'.

Film projectors became available for a few schools. Textbooks began to replace the teacher's 'lecture' in many subjects. Classroom walls displayed illustrations produced by both the teacher and the pupils. Free school meals were provided in many towns for children with unemployed parents. School milk was provided in 1934 and it was either free or extremely cheap.

As with so many other matters, education between 1919–39 made disappointingly little progress because of money shortages. Only twelve per cent of children went to secondary schools in 1924. By 1937 this had only increased to a mere 19 per cent. More than half the parents of these children paid fees for secondary places. Higher education also suffered. Although new universities were established at Reading, Swansea, Leicester and Hull only four children out of every 1,000 in the old elementary schools eventually reached one of these or one of the older establishments such as London, Birmingham or Leeds Universities. The plans made for education in the late 1930's including, once again, the raising of the school-leaving age to 15, were inevitably put into 'cold storage' when war broke out in September 1939.

Law and Order

After the First World War the number of crimes reported to the police began to increase, the increase being particularly rapid after 1930. People began to talk of a 'crime wave'. The greatest increase was in crimes against property, which included both stealing and robbery with violence. Between 1908–13 there were about 12,000 or 13,000 'crimes against property involving violence' each year. In the 1920's there were about 18,000 and in the 1930's about 35,000 each year. Offences of theft rose from 70,000 to 80,000 before the war to over 100,000 in the early 1930's and to 200,000 by the late 1930's.

One new type of crime which developed during this period involved the use of motor cars. The most obvious crime was stealing someone else's car. Many men, according to a prison governor, had learnt about motor vehicles in the army and wanted to continue driving after the war, even if it meant stealing.

One American also believed that because motoring was so costly, some men had to steal to get the extra cash. By 1935 almost 4,000 cars a year were being stolen in London. Many had their number plates changed and after being repainted, were sold off. There were many new offences which motorists could commit while driving, as new controls and regulations were imposed (see page 120).

Policemen take to the air

Whilst the 'Chicago-gangster' type of crime, involving wild car chases and sub-machine guns was almost unknown in Britain there was an increase in 'break-ins' of houses in the rich suburb around London. 'The travelling criminal is all over the country,' said an Assistant Commissioner at Scotland Yard.

Frauds and confidence tricks were another class of crime which grew rapidly. The number of malicious woundings rose from around 500 to 1,500 a year over this period and the number of manslaughters from about 100 to 170. The murder rate remained remarkably steady at about 100 a year. Nevertheless, some murder cases, involving the cutting up of the victim's bodies, provided the newspapers with a good deal of sensational material.

At the end of the First World War the police force, particularly in London, was not a happy profession. The cost of living rose rapidly and whereas many workers secured large pay rises, the police fell far behind. Many policemen got into debt or even took second jobs. Most worked every day, often on a split-shift system: four hours on duty, four hours rest, four hours duty. In protest many policemen joined the National Union of Police and Prison Officers.

The end result of this situation was that on 30th August 1918 almost every policeman in London went on strike. Lloyd George was forced to act. Troops took up positions in important places in the capital and watched by cheering strikers the union leaders went into 10 Downing Street. A large pay increase was given and the policemen went back on duty. The Cabinet realised that changes were needed in the police and appointed the tough General Macready to take charge of the Metropolitan Police. Macready brought in many reforms and another pay rise. The result was that when a second strike was called in July 1919 it was ignored by all but 1,100 of London's 19,000 policemen. In Liverpool the situation was more serious. Half the city's force struck and although the government sent the battleship *Valiant* and 700 men from Midlands regiments, there were two nights of looting and vicious street fighting between the mobs on one hand and the remaining police, troops and special constables on the other.

After these upheavals the police settled down to deal with the 'crime wave'. To meet the threat of criminals in cars, Scotland Yard formed its own 'flying squad' in 1919 equipped with fast cars. The following year saw wireless sets first used to give better contact between control rooms and mobile units. Policewomen, first enrolled in 1918, became a permanent part of most forces. Britain also joined the international police organisation, Interpol, formed to track down criminals who fled to other countries. At the Police College at Hendon in Middlesex a scheme began in 1933 to train bright young men for the highest posts in the force. The plan was abandoned after a few years.

It was certainly necessary for Britain's police to be alert and intelligent, for in addition to fighting the ordinary criminal, they had new and difficult tasks to face. Drug-peddling, particularly in the areas around the large ports, increased during the 1920's. As the drugs came from Asia it was convenient to blame such groups as the Chinese. Another sensational type of crime for which the Chinese, amongst others, were blamed, was the disappearance of girls, taken abroad it was believed, as 'white slaves'.

Political groups, using a variety of methods to gain their ends, were also a serious challenge. The Irish Republican Army, dissatisfied with the terms of Irish independence (1922) resorted to terror which included a spate of bombings in 1939. The British Communist Party, believed to be using Russian money to cause strikes and marches of the unemployed, was raided in 1925. Fortunately one of the major disputes, the 1926 General Strike, went off without bloodshed. The good relations between police and strikers were demonstrated in Plymouth by a football match.

Less peaceful in their methods than the strikers were the members of the British Union of Fascists who were organised under a former Labour M.P., Sir Oswald Mosley. The Fascists, in imitation of Mussolini, wore black shirts and, in imitation of Hitler, attacked Jewish shops. In 1936, disturbed by the unrest at Fascist meetings,

Parliament passed the Public Order Act banning the wearing of military style uniforms.

In spite of these troubles, the police remained popular. Certainly with between one million and three million unemployed there was no shortage of recruits. Although policemen were killed on duty, Britain between the wars was still generally a law-abiding country.

The Nation's Health

There is little doubt that health standards rose rapidly between the wars. Millions of young men were medically examined for service in the armed forces between 1917 and 1918. Only 36 per cent were found to be perfectly fit and healthy, whilst 41 per cent were either totally unfit or suffering from some serious disability. In 1939–45, using the same standards, several million more men were examined. This time 70 per cent were put into the top grade and only 16 per cent in the two bottom grades. The same improvement applied to children. Ten-year-old children in one large city were found to be about 3 in (7·62 cm) taller and 9 lb (4 kg) heavier in 1938 than children of the same age in 1920. The number of children who died during their first year fell by one-third between 1921–35, as did the number of tuberculosis deaths during the same period. Deaths from cancer and heart disease, however, continued to rise steadily. These generally attacked older people.

There were many reasons for this improvement in the nation's health. The most important was probably the fall in food prices. The great farming nations of the world produced much more food than they could sell. As a result the overall cost of food in

Britain fell by 30 per cent between 1925 and 1933. At the same time, wages continued to rise and even in hard-hit industries there were no massive wage cuts after the defeat of the miners' strike in 1926.

Better quality food was eaten by most people. This included more meat, fish, eggs and milk. By 1934 most education authorities were providing free milk or at a very low price. The school meals service spread to many more areas providing free dinners (and sometimes breakfast and teas) to the poorer children. Whilst eating habits improved, drunkenness declined. This was partly because of unemployment but also because the cinema house and the B.B.C. offered more for the customer's money than did the pub. The house-building boom took people out of smoky insanitary slum areas into the healthier suburbs.

Medical services were also considerably improved during this period. The National Health Insurance Act of 1911 covered 15 million persons by 1921 and 20 million by 1938. Not only did the birth-rate fall, enabling mothers to rest more and give each child more attention, but more than 3,500 welfare clinics for infants and nearly 1,800 ante-natal clinics were opened between 1918 and 1938. Children at school received more attention, if not treatment, from medical officers and dentists.

Yet it would be quite misleading to think that everyone was well provided for. The unemployed and their families who numbered between three and ten million persons, did not actually starve but if they bought any little luxuries these had to be paid for by smaller meals. Those living in a new council house who became unemployed found it particularly difficult both to eat well and pay the higher rent. Many took in lodgers or even moved back to the cheaper slums. One survey in 1936 claimed that only 30 per cent of the nation were eating a really adequate diet and that 10 per cent were very badly fed. This last figure meant 4,500,000 people.

National Health Insurance did not cover wives, except when pregnant, nor the under-14s. Free medical treatment was available either in the Poor Law hospitals (transferred to local councils in 1930) or voluntary hospitals. The latter found it was very difficult to keep going. In spite of flag days and small weekly contributions from workers many had to close wards or borrow from their bank.

The poorer sections of the community, particularly the unemployed, did suffer ill-health more severely.

Long periods of idleness made men physically and mentally unfit for work. Their wives and children suffered from anaemia and

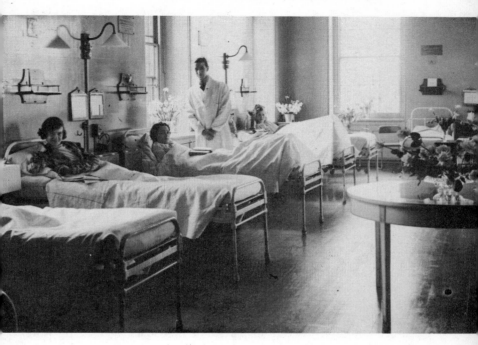

A hospital in the 1930's

minor ailments; the former were most at risk during pregnancy. Very few people became either insane or attempted suicide unless there were other important factors. The rates of serious illness, such as pneumonia and tuberculosis were, however, much higher in the 'distressed areas' such as South Wales and the North East than in the more prosperous areas. The food was poorer, the housing damper and more overcrowded. Also the local councils were often too short of money to pay for new drainage schemes or the replacement of privies by modern water-closets.

Medical scientists working in laboratories throughout the world did offer more hope for the future. The most important discoveries were in the field of antibiotic drugs. In 1928 Alexander Fleming isolated the mould which was to become known as penicillin. In 1935 the 'sulphonamide' drugs, which successfully attacked a variety of diseases, including pneumonia, began to be produced. For the children of the 1920's and 1930's at least, both the then present and the future seemed to hold the brightest opportunities.

Social Security

The 1911 National Insurance Act had been partly designed to protect 2 million workers in particular industries against the worst effects of temporary unemployment. The Act was extended in 1916 and in 1920 it covered 11 million workers, but not railwaymen, domestic and civil servants, agricultural workers, policemen and those earning more than £250 per year. The amount of benefit was sufficient to prevent starvation, if used wisely, but it made little provision for new clothes, furniture, entertainments or the little luxuries which make life more bearable. In 1927 a single man received 17s (85p) per week. If he was married with three children he received an extra 13s (65p). Women received 2s (10p) a week less than men whilst a 16-year-old unemployed boy could expect 6s (30p).

Soon after the passing of the 1920 Act, unemployment in Britain began to increase rapidly. By the summer of 1921 there were more than 2 million out of work and although this figure fell it remained above the 1 million mark until 1940. In 1931–3 it was above 2 and even 3 million. Amongst these unemployed it was discovered that about 500,000 were long-term unemployed. These were mainly men over 40 who had been coal-miners, shipyard, metallurgical or textile workers in the distressed areas. Another 800,000, for example seaside workers during the winter or coalminers in the more profitable coalfields during summer, were subject to seasonal unemployment. There were also about 100,000 men in such industries as buildings and public works who suffered longer periods of unemployment at longer intervals.

The 1920 Act and those which followed all tried to preserve the idea of insurance. This meant that a man paid in small amounts over a long period and drew out sums during the short time he would be out of work. Briefly, insurance was to be the bridge across the abyss of unemployment. Thousands of workers exhausted their 15-weeks' 'unemployment benefit' and the bridge had to be lengthened for them and their families through the provision of 'extended' or 'transitional' benefit. To prevent the insurance fund running dry the Treasury had to pump in ever-increasing amounts. Nevertheless, by 1928 the fund was in debt by £25 million and successive governments ordered inquiries into its operation. Several changes were made and in 1928 a new Act came into force to make it easier for the unemployed to draw benefit. Even so, by mid-1929 the number of people out of work began increasing rapidly until it reached 20 per cent. If more than six per cent were unemployed the insurance fund began to get into debt.

Inevitably there were many thousands who did not qualify for unemployment pay or were 'struck off' for various reasons. In addition, there were many more thousands who through age, infirmity or the loss of the breadwinner were threatened with destitution. All these people, including many mentally sick persons, came under the care of the Poor Law Guardians. Each town or group of parishes formed a Poor Law Union set up by the 1834 Act.

The Guardians had the power to levy rates. This money could be spent as in-relief by putting the destitute into the workhouse or Poor Law hospital. Alternatively, the Guardians could make cash payments which were usually slightly less than Government unemployment benefit. The areas with the heaviest unemployment could least afford the heaviest Poor Law rates. In order to meet the demands of times such as the 1926 Coal Dispute many unions had to borrow from the Ministry of Health. By 1927 the West Ham Union owed £2·275 million, and Bedwellty in South Wales £1 million to the Ministry. The Poor Law Unions, which were feared and detested by most people had never been designed to support 400,000 unemployed as they were doing in the 1920's. By the Local Government Act of 1929 they were drastically altered. Their place was taken by Public Assistance Committees from April 1930 and the other duties of the Guardians were assigned to other departments of the local councils. The Public Assistance Committee still obtained most of its monies from the local rates, so that local unemployment could still be an enormous local burden. In 1933-4 Sheffield spent 7s 4d (36½p) out of each £1 rates on public assistance.

Meanwhile a Royal Commission on Unemployment Insurance had been set up in 1930 to reconstruct completely the administration of the fund. It reported in 1932 and a new Act came into force on 1st January 1935. This Act was much too late to prevent drastic changes through the 1931 Economy Act which removed 180,000 persons from benefit within a year and imposed a searching examination—the 'means test'—on those making a claim. This included the earnings of other members of the family, so that if a father was out of work and his children were earning they might be forced to support him.

The Unemployment Act of 1934 instituted a central Unemployment Assistance Board which took over responsibility for all able-bodied unemployed. At first it paid less than many had been getting from the Public Assistance Committees but the cuts were later restored. By 1937 only about 35,000 unemployed were still being cared for by public assistance.

A full-time staff of 6,000 was recruited to administer the new service. Fortunately, after 1934 the employment situation improved and the Board was never in danger of getting into debt. In 1939 it took over responsibility for war victims as well.

Old Age Pensions (introduced in 1908) were increased to 10s (50p) per week in 1919 but were still not paid until the age of 70. In 1927 however, the Widows, Orphans and Old Age Contributory Pensions Act came into force. It provided 10s (50p) a week for widows plus a children's allowance. Orphans received 7s 6d (37½p) per week and workers and their wives had earlier pensions of 10s (50p) per week at the age of 65.

SOCIAL SECURITY SPENDING
(£ MILLION)

	1910		1925		1935
Poor	12.4	Poor	31.4	Poor	34.3
Old Age Pensions	8.5	Pensions	94.8	Pensions	98.0
Housing	0.6	Housing	18.1	Housing	42.3
		Unemployment	16.9	Unemployment	73.9
		Health Insurance	21.1	Health Insurance	25.7
	21.5		182.3		274.2

Leisure

The reduction of the number of hours worked each week and the spread of short-time working and unemployment meant that millions of men and women had far more spare time available than their parents and grandparents ever had. Indeed, for the unemployed one of their biggest problems was to prevent boredom.

A great deal of time was spent at home, particularly if the weather was bad. The morning paper cost 1d ($\frac{1}{2}$p) and there was great competition amongst the 'dailies' for new readers. Free gifts, life insurance and competitions were one means. Serialised stories were also used. Public libraries were also very popular and new branches opened in the suburbs were soon very busy. Mobile libraries began to serve the villages. Reading was particularly popular amongst the unemployed because it cost almost nothing.

Undoubtedly the greatest new form of entertainment at home was radio broadcasting. This had begun in 1920 from the Marconi Company's station at Chelmsford, but in 1922 it was decided that one organisation was to be founded for this purpose, the British Broadcasting Company. On 20th December 1926, under the leadership of J. C. W. Reith (later Lord Reith) the British Broadcasting Corporation was formed. In 1927 regional programmes were added. A crystal set receiver could be made for as little as 1s (5p) but whether this or a factory-made set were used a licence was required.

A Manchester cinema. 1938

By 1932 over 4·3 million licences had been issued, but probably an equal number of people did not bother to buy them, despite the prosecution of offenders after 1926. News programmes, educational talks, plays and serious music were prominent features amongst the B.B.C.'s productions. These could be supplemented by enrolling at the increasing number of night school classes which were available in most towns. Experimental television programmes were made in 1929 but only a few thousand people in the London area were able to watch with any regularity during the last few years before the Second World War.

Outside the home the cinema was much the most popular of all entertainments. During most of the 1920's all films were silent and by 1929 there were more than 3,000 cinemas throughout the country. Most films were American, but in 1927 Parliament passed the Cinematograph Films Act which required cinema programmes eventually to consist of 20 per cent of British films. These were made at Elstree and Shepherd's Bush in London and many were of poor quality. In 1928 the first full-length 'talkie' was made (in the U.S.A.) and attendances improved. By 1935 Britain had 4,300 cinemas and most seats were less than 7d (3p) with some as cheap as 2p (1p). Unemployment and a special entertainments tax reduced attendance after 1931, but the cinema still offered more value for money than public houses and theatres. By the mid-1930's some 20 million cinema tickets were sold each week for a total of nearly £800,000. New 'super-cinemas', Odeons and Gaumonts, were built in the centres of the larger towns but of course few of their

1,500 or so seats were cheap. Nevertheless, even in Liverpool, which had 90,000 unemployed in 1932, 40 per cent of the population went once a week, and 25 per cent twice a week, to one of the 69 cinemas in the city. Few could blame people living in miserable surroundings for seeking a few hours' escape and adventure in the 'front stalls'.

For the young and energetic there were plenty of opportunities for sport. Association football was by far the most popular winter game. There were nearly 750 registered football clubs in the Sheffield region alone in 1927. Most towns and villages had parks and recreation grounds where it was possible to have a 'kick-around'. Rugby Union in South Wales and Rugby League in Lancashire and Yorkshire attracted a large following, but the support received was considerably less than that of the big Football League Clubs, Arsenal, Aston Villa, Manchester City and Newcastle United. Attendances at Division I games frequently exceeded 60,000 and when Wembley stadium opened in 1923 over 200,000 persons tried to get to see the Cup Final. In 1927 the B.B.C. gave the first live radio commentary of the game. The crowds dropped only as a result of high unemployment in certain cities. The first World Cup tournament held in far-off Uruguay in 1930 attracted little attention in

Television, 1938

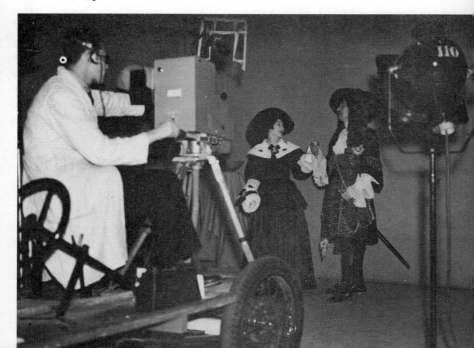

Britain; neither did most athletics meetings except during the four-yearly Olympic Games and the 1934 Empire Games in London.

Cricket remained the supreme summer sport, attracting hundreds of thousands of spectators and players. The largest crowds were reserved for the visiting Australians in 1926, 1930, 1934 and 1938. Boxing was also followed with the greatest interest. World championship fights were described round-by-round on the front pages of the papers; but at the local level open-air contests, sometimes free but with a collection made, drew 8,000–10,000 spectators. The number of active boxers was small by comparison with the numbers in football or cricket. There was no shortage of strong youngsters ready to avoid the 'dole' queues by way of the boxing ring.

Two completely new spectator sports which grew up in the 1920's and 1930's were speedway and greyhound racing. Speedway racing flourished in the period 1933–9 when the Belle Vue team dominated the National League and Cup. Greyhound racing began in Manchester in 1926.

By 1932 the 187 stadia were attracting more than 15 million spectators, many of whom paid only 7d (3p) admission. The big attraction was betting, which replaced drink as the 'greatest public evil'. By The Racecourse Betting Act of 1928, gambling on horses was made legal and that on dogs soon afterwards. About £220 million went on bets in 1929. Scores of special trains and buses carried punters to the big race meetings at Ascot, Aintree and Doncaster. Unemployed men went even if it meant a 15-mile (24 km) walk each day. Football pools began in the 1920's as newspaper competitions on match results. By 1936 the well-known pools firms were well established with six million clients and with 10 million by 1938, spending £40 million a year. For a stake of 6d (2½p) a top dividend of £22,000 could be won. One result was 30,000 new jobs, many in the unemployment black-spot of Liverpool.

Hiking and cycling became extremely popular amongst young people, especially in the large northern cities. To enable longer trips to be undertaken cheap accommodation was provided by the Youth Hostels Association with 12 hostels opening in 1931. By 1938 the Y.H.A. had 83,000 members visiting its 300 hostels which were mainly in the mountainous areas of Britain. Holiday-making was also made more widely possible by the Holidays with Pay Act 1938 which applied to 11 million workers. One result was the building of holiday camps. The first opened at Skegness in 1937; by 1939 there

Whitsuntide 1937—girl hikers

were more than 100. For those unable to take a full week off coach companies and the railways laid on numerous holiday excursions at 1d ($\frac{1}{2}$p) a mile (1·6 km) or less. On Easter Monday and Whit-Monday the platforms at the large railway stations were eight or nine deep with day-trippers. On August Bank Holiday Monday 1928 Sheffield Midland station was described as a 'struggling mass of humanity' as 40,000 people attempted to leave the city.

Drinking and drunkenness decreased after 1920, possibly as a result of high unemployment but also because of the attractions of other forms of entertainments, especially radio and the cinema. The demolition of slums also reduced the number of public houses whilst the great new housing estates were frequently 'dry'. The number of licensed premises fell from almost 89,000 in 1913 to less than 78,000 in 1930 whilst beer consumption fell by about 40 per cent and convictions for drunkenness by nearly 80 per cent.

The Middle Classes

The economic depression amongst the older 'nineteenth-century' industries (coal, cotton, etc.) of the north and west of Britain and the rise of light science-based industries and services in the South East created a 'population drift'. People moved to find work. Thus between 1921–38 the population of South East England increased by 18 per cent (2½ million) and that of the Midlands by 11·6 per cent (nearly 1 million). By contrast, the population of South Wales fell by 8 per cent, the rest of Wales by nearly 5 per cent and the North East by 1 per cent. These changes reduced by about 900,000 the number of persons working in primary industries such as coal, textiles and iron and steel and increased by 2 million the numbers in tertiary industries such as banking, the civil service, insurance and the learned professions. The latter group, who are often referred to as 'white collar' workers, are paid annual salaries instead of a weekly (or hourly) wage. The receipt of an annual salary is one of the qualifications for being considered 'middle class'.

The growth of the salaried classes was particularly remarkable between 1911 and 1921. In the former year they were 1·7 million (12 per cent of the work force). By the latter year the number had risen to 2·7 million (22 per cent) and by 1931 to almost 3 million. During the inter-war period the percentage of persons earning salaries rose about two and a half times faster than the number of wage earners. Even though 'white-collar' jobs were thought to be very safe, many such people did become unemployed. One estimate in 1930 was 500,000, but this was probably a temporary situation for most. What is certain is that the salaried worker's income was consistently 25 per cent higher than the wage-earner's during this period.

This meant that salaried 'white-collar' workers were much better placed to buy one of the millions of new houses being built at this time. Building societies greatly increased their lending, and interest rates were only about five per cent in the 1930's but they were happier to lend to a salaried clerk or a skilled mechanic than to a low-paid unskilled worker.

If the new middle-class could easily buy houses, they could not afford the pre-1914 numbers of domestic servants. For one reason taxation rates were twice as high in 1938 as they were in 1913. Also, women preferred other types of work to the often strict discipline, long hours and low pay of the domestic servant. By 1931 only one household in twenty throughout Britain had a resident domestic although the number was much higher (two in five) in wealthy areas such as the West End of London. The growth of the electrical goods industry which produced washing machines, vacuum cleaners and irons made many household tasks easier. The houses of the middle-class were also very much smaller than before 1914.

The purchase of household goods and luxury items was made possible partly by the rapid growth of hire-purchase. Some £50 million worth of credit was made available by the 1930's and again the salaried middle-class worker in a safe job was usually able to take the best advantage of it. Certainly if he hoped to buy a car he would need some form of credit. Car ownership rose rapidly from over 300,000 in 1922 to a million in 1930 and two million in 1939. Mass production methods reduced prices until it was possible to buy a new car ready for the road for slightly more than £110. By the mid-1930's the amount of traffic in the big cities and the annual death toll of around 7,000 produced new laws to try to improve road safety.

The growth of family motoring trips, particularly on Sundays, was one of the developments blamed for the fall in church attendances. In fact the majority of people in modern Britain had never been regular churchgoers. After the First World War and all its horrors men seemed less inclined to find comfort in religion. The churches themselves experienced changes and difficulties. The Church of England, faced with increasing money shortage both to pay its clergy and to repair old churches, had to launch fresh appeals to build new churches in the great housing estates. The three largest Methodist Churches united in 1932, following the example of the Scottish Presbyterians in 1929. The Roman Catholic Church helped by a steady flow of Irish immigrants and a number of important converts such as G. K. Chesterton, survived the period well.

The decline in religion was paralleled by the increasing liberation of women. Those over 30 years of age gained the vote in 1918 and the 21-year-olds ten years later. The freedom of jobs achieved by women during the war was largely maintained except in the heavy industries. At the same time the slaughter in the trenches increased the existing 'surplus' of women. It therefore became accepted that single middle-class women worked, smoked, drank and went around without a chaperone. Moreover, they wore fashions which would have caused the Victorians to shudder. In 1915 the hemline began to rise and by 1926 had passed over the knee, only to begin its descent again. Sports clothes were similarly affected and hair was worn short. Men's fashions, although becoming more relaxed, did not change so dramatically.

A group of ladies at the Henley Regatta, 1926

The emancipation of married women was assisted by and reflected in the continued fall in the birth rate. Apart from a brief spell in 1920–1 following the large number of post-war marriages, the number of live births fell below a million in 1916. By 1933 it had fallen below 700,000, at which level it remained until 1943. Contraception techniques which had long been limited to the highest groups spread down through society. Amongst the unemployed illegal abortions were a common method of preventing an increase in family size. Certainly after 1920 the two- or three-child family became the norm.

Social
Investigation

With 1, 2 and even 3 million unemployed between 1921-39, it became obvious that British society was suffering from many troubles. The miners in 1926 tried to save their position by long and bitter strikes. Thousands joined the Communist and Fascist parties in the belief that ruthless methods were needed to save the country. Many thoughtful men and women investigated different aspects of society. In particular they tried to find out why there was so much unemployment, hunger and misery at a time when most people were better off than ever before. The Government also ordered surveys to be made of the most difficult problems, such as the distressed areas. These were carried out by universities and colleges close to the areas in question.

Although investigators could not fully agree on how to measure 'poverty' or 'malnutrition' all found that not less than ten per cent of the population were 'very poor'. This meant they had so little income that their health and ability to work were seriously affected. Even in towns like Bristol, a centre of the growing aviation industry, and York were hiding large groups 'below the poverty line'. The figure was well above 10 per cent in the distressed areas such as South Wales and the north east where between 60 and 95 per cent of men might be unemployed.

The investigators also found three major causes of poverty. These were old age, unemployment and membership of a large family. Of the three, unemployment was the most serious, since for every man unemployed there were probably two or three people dependent on him.

To be poor as a result of unemployment meant living in low-standard housing. To be allocated a new council house required a minimum income higher than the 'dole'. Those who became unemployed after obtaining a council house either took in lodgers or returned to the slums. The poor could never afford new furniture or clothes. Jumble-sales, charities or needle-work classes provided the latter. Entertainment was confined to a 3d (1p) seat in the cinema, perhaps once a fortnight.

The most serious result of being poor was found to be the lack of good food. Children suffered least because more and more schools were providing school meals and, after 1934, free milk. In Sheffield the Schools Medical Officers found only 0·5 per cent of children 'badly fed'. Married men who were out of work dared not neglect their food lest they became too weak and ill to seize the chance of a job if one became vacant. The greatest sufferers were the mothers. Between 1925 and 1934 the number of women dying in childbirth, as a result of under-nourishment and lack of medical attention, rose steadily. The largest numbers of these deaths were found to be in the towns with high unemployment.

The most detailed study into the state of nutrition was published in 1936. The title was *Food, Health and Income* and its author Sir John Boyd Orr.

The budgets of 1,152 families were studied and it was decided to define a completely adequate diet as producing 'a state of well-being such that no improvement can be effected by a change in diet'. Boyd-Orr then divided the population into six groups and found that only 30 per cent of the population enjoyed a perfectly adequate diet. Ten per cent, whose weekly expenditure per head on food was less than 4s (20p), had a diet lacking in all important constituents (proteins, minerals, vitamins, fats and calories). The remaining 60 per cent were lacking something or other from their diets which was important to their health. Not everyone accepted these findings, but even if they were exaggerated it was perfectly clear that serious pockets of poverty and hunger did exist and that only some action by the Government could eradicate them.

Agriculture

To meet the U-boat threat to Britain's imported food supplies during the First World War, the Government urged farmers to increase food production. The Corn Production Act of 1917 protected the farmers against losses and also established minimum wages for farm labourers. The farmers responded by ploughing up an extra million hectares. By 1918 U.K. corn production at 4·16 million tonnes was about 32 per cent higher than the 1913 figure. Potato production went up by 60 per cent.

In 1920 Government assistance was continued through the Agriculture Act. At this moment corn prices had reached their highest level of the century so the farmers needed no financial help. Then prices began to tumble. Wheat fell from £4·32 a quarter in 1920 to £2·04 in 1922. The reason was simply over-production. Canada, Argentina and the U.S.A. had all greatly increased their agricultural output, supplying much of Europe's food requirements. The British blockade and German U-boat campaign then forced European farmers to increase their production. The farmers of the 'New World' were thus left with an unsaleable surplus.

The British Government was worried more by its own than by the farmers' financial troubles.

The annual cost of propping up agricultural prices would have exceeded £20 million. In 1921 Parliament abandoned its support for the farmers. Agricultural prices continued to fall

Forestry Commission workers preparing to plant, 1931

throughout much of the world until 1933 after which they began to rise again. This meant that food prices and therefore the cost of living fell, probably saving a lot of unemployed men and their families from real hunger. For the farmer and the farm worker this meant a struggle to keep going. Many gave up. Nearly 40 per cent of the land producing cereals in 1919 had either been abandoned or turned to pasture by 1938. The corn crop fell from 3 to 1·8 million tonnes between the same years while imports, mostly from Canada and Australia, rose by half.

The farm labourer, for long one of the worst paid of workers, naturally suffered severely during the agricultural depression. In 1919 the agricultural worker's wage of 42s (£2.10) had fallen within a few years to 28s (£1.40). This was almost exactly half the pay of a building labourer. In March 1923 there was even a strike in Norfolk amongst 6,000 farm workers which was settled by bargaining. Low wages were not the only complaint of the farm worker. Many thousands lived in tied cottages. These were owned by the farmer and went with the job. Tied cottages were frequently very old, cramped and damp. It was most unlikely that, even by 1939, they would be supplied with electricity, piped water or a mains sewage system. Despite the development of rural bus services, which also helped to close 1,000 miles of railway branch lines, few farm workers or their families were able to enjoy a full social life. The village pub and the Women's Institute would be the most common source of leisure.

Inevitably poor pay and conditions and a depressed market caused many to look for work elsewhere. In 1920 agriculture and forestry employed more than one million persons. By 1938 the figure was little more than 700,000.

Yet it would be wrong to imagine that the countryside of

Britain decayed completely while the Government looked on uncaring. In 1919 the Forestry Commission was set up to replace the timber hastily felled during the war.

By 1939 it had spent £9 million and begun plantings in a total area the size of Lancashire or Essex. Acts of Parliament were passed to lend money to farmers who wanted to improve their lands and machinery and to men who wanted to set up smallholdings. Very large subsidies were given to set up a sugar beet industry. This proved a very expensive way of encouraging a new crop even if it provided thousands of new jobs in one of the 17 new factories in East Anglia.

By 1931, as the world economic depression set in, the British Government was forced to take even more drastic measures to protect agriculture (and other industries). Subsidies were given to wheat growers guaranteeing a minimum price of 45s (£2.25) per quarter up to a maximum of 1.35 million tonnes. Import duties were also charged on an increasing range of foreign foodstuffs. Thus British farmers found wheat-growing more profitable and ploughed up 200,000 hectares between 1931–7. The Agricultural Marketing Act of 1933 set up boards to advise farmers and control output and prices of potatoes (1934), milk (1933) and bacon (1933). These protections and subsidies granted to British farmers cost well over £30 million per year. Additionally they affected the economies of countries which, like Denmark and Argentina, relied on exports to Britain.

Agricultural productivity also increased in the 1930's. The increasing use of tractors was one reason. By 1939 over 50,000 were in use on British farms. Agricultural research stations discovered new means of pest control and of improving crop yields. Combine harvesters were tried out on some 150 of the larger farms. The B.B.C. played its part by putting out talks and bulletins for farmers.

Basically, agriculture presented a number of complex problems. The British wanted cheap food but the cheapest food came from overseas. The British farmer wanted a good living, but he could not compete with the foreign produce unless he received either protection or massive subsidies. The Government could not let domestic agriculture collapse and particularly from 1937 when the possibility of war once again loomed large. The Government, therefore, had to support the farmer, but not to such an extent that he had no incentive to increase his productivity. At the same time imported foods could not be drastically cut down. Otherwise Britain, the world's greatest food importer, would have been unable to sell her manufactures to the impoverished food-producing nations.

As with so many other problems, the problem of agriculture was pushed into the background by the outbreak of the Second World War in September 1939. The renewed threat of the submarine once again led to official encouragement to the farmers to produce as much as possible.

Documents

The Industrial Worker, 1918–39

The miseries of inter-war unemployment as seen by contemporaries.
Quoted in James Laver, Britain Between the Wars *(London, 1961) pp. 137–41.*

'There are men of forty-five and even less who have to face a future without hope of regular employment. A few months ago I was in a northern district where such "elderly" unemployed abound and where, accordingly, a centre had been started to give them occupation and interest; when I enquired what was the age of qualification for admission to membership, I was told that the rule was, no member under thirty-five! Thirty-five—and no likelihood of permanent employment . . . The plain fact being that, in England of today, many men and women are only past work because the work is not there for them to take.'

Cicely Hamilton, 'Modern England', 1938

¶ The situation was particularly bad in South Wales:
'I gazed out of my hotel bedroom at P—— in South Wales. The sight . . . was one of the most doleful I have ever seen in my life. It consisted chiefly of this: Men—obviously dressed in their Sunday best—standing with their hands in their pockets along the street kerb. Just standing . . . I knew that if I asked some of them, they would tell me they were "waiting for something to pass by"—a chance to run an errand, or do something to earn a few pence. Others, especially the men over thirty-five (and they are becoming bitter realists now) would answer they were waiting for the Old Age Pension to come along.
'These were some of the 15,000 hale, hearty, and capable miners of X (a population of about 104,000 people) who will probably never go down a mine shaft again in their lives. A problematical chance of improved markets will be met by

nationalisation; and it was the conclusion of practically every one I talked with in that "valley of despair" that, unless there is found some way to drain them off, there will always remain about that number of unemployed . . . One man when I asked him what he looked forward to said: "I am just lingering. That's it—lingering."

'There is one question, especially after you have been among them for a time, that you will never ask these miners in South Wales; and that is whether they would rather work or live on the Dole. That peculiar dead-alive look in their faces as they stand in the streets is enough to save you from that.'

'The Sphere', February 28th, 1931

¶ It was equally deplorable in the North, in places like Jarrow:

'When I visited Jarrow in the depth of its worklessness it was not for the first time; I knew the Tyneside well in my younger days, when all along the river you were never out of hearing of the clang, clang, clang, of hammers from the shipyard. At the best of times—the busiest and the most prosperous—Jarrow was not an attractive place for the stranger; its streets had been built in response to the industrial needs of the nineteenth century and were as dreary and grubby-looking as most of the streets that were built at that period, for that purpose. But when I first knew it there was bustle of activity in those dreary, grubby streets; men going about their work, women going about their shopping, the baker and the grocer busy with their customers; a squalid town like so many in the north, but alive!

'On my last visit I was taken to see an exhibit in urban lifelessness; a street which had once been a shopping centre of the town, tenanted by bakers and grocers and drapers, and where now almost every trader had despaired and put up his shutters. It reminded me of some deserted town in the war zone; there were back streets in it that looked much like that when I saw them shortly after the Armistice. Between thirty and forty, I think, was the number of shops that had closed in that little street; their shutters the outward and visible sign of broken homes and hopes.'

Cicely Hamilton, 'Modern England', 1938

¶ Some of the individual stories make very sad reading:

'A SKILLED ENGINEER'S TRAGEDY

'I am an engineer by trade, forty-seven years of age, married and the father of one child. Until four years ago I worked for a large engineering firm in the North Midlands. I had worked for this firm for many years, but owing to loss of contracts the firm was compelled to close down and I found myself unemployed for the first time in my life. Up to this time I had lived the life of an ordinary respectable artisan. I earned the standard rate of wage, round about £3 a week, and maintained a decent house at a rent of 15s. 3d. I have been happily married some twenty years and was devoted to my wife and child. My activities were divided between home, garden and public affairs. I had held every office possible in my trade union branch. I took a keen interest in politics both locally and nationally.

'During the first months of unemployment I felt confident in being able to find another job. I received unemployment pay and a few shillings weekly from my trade union. But the trade union's funds were low and this latter source of income ceased after a few months. Nevertheless, by the aid of our little savings we were able to get along . . .

'After a year of vain efforts I decided to accept any job I could get . . . but I soon found that outside my trade I could get nothing . . . In the meantime my wife . . . obtained a job as house to house saleswoman, and was able to earn a few shillings to supplement our dole income. It was from this time that the feeling of strain which was beginning to appear in our home life became more marked . . . Life became more and more strained. There were constant bickerings over money matters . . . The final blow came when the Means Test was put into operation . . . Quarrels broke out anew and bitter things were said. Eventually, after the most heartbreaking period of my life, both my wife and son, who had just commenced to earn a few shillings, told me to get out, as I was living on them and taking the food they needed.

'I left and took with me a little furniture. I rented an unfurnished bedroom for 4s. 6d. a week in the house of an unemployed man who had a wife and three children. This happened some fifteen months ago. Since then I have drawn 15s. 3d. weekly from the dole and have had to sell every bit of furniture I had . . . and try to exist on 8s. od. a week for food. I have never been able to afford coal for a fire . . . The outlook as far as I am concerned is hopeless. I've given up dreaming of any return to my former life and work, and just hang on hoping something big will happen before I die.'

H. L. Beales and R. S. Lambert, 'Memoirs of the Unemployed',
1934

¶ That was the tragedy. The unemployed gradually became unemployable:

'The moral fibre of the unemployed cannot resist either the life they are now leading, or the complacency with which it is accepted. A feeling of slackness pervades the atmosphere; inspectors report that they often find the inveterate unemployed stretched out in bed during the day. For these leftovers, hour follows hour with nothing to do except an occasional visit to the Labour Exchange to see if by chance there is a job to be had. Finally, all effort, aptitude, and energy are benumbed.'

André Siegfried, 'England's Crisis', 1931

¶ A young poet gave poignant expression to the prevailing despair:

'Moving through the silent crowd
Who stand behind dull cigarettes,
These men who idle in the road,
I have the sense of falling light.

'They lounge at corners of the street
And greet friends with a shrug of shoulder
And turn their empty pockets out,
The cynical gesture of the poor.

'Now they've no work, like better men
Who sit at desks and take much pay,
They sleep long nights and rise at ten
To watch the hours that drain away.

'I'm jealous of the weeping hours
They stare through with such hungry eyes.
I'm haunted by these images,
I'm haunted by their emptiness.'

Stephen Spender, 'Collected Poems,' 1955

¶ This, however sincere, was the outsider's view. Here is another account from one of those actually affected:

'A SOUTH WALES MINER

'It was in June 1927, that I first began to draw unemployment benefit at the rate of £1 9s. od. a week. At that time my eldest boy, who was then fifteen, had not started work as he could not find a job . . . until at last the manager of one colliery told him he would give him a start because he was ashamed to keep turning him away. He is still working at the same colliery . . . his wages being 15s. a week, which made our income up to £2 4s. od. and enabled us to buy him some clothes. After paying our rent we still had £1 15s. od. a week to live on. Then my second son came out of school and found he could not get work, but he went to the training centre and there eventually got work. His wage was 15s. too, so that we had £2 10s. od. after allowing for rent . . .

'My unemployment benefit came to an end in March, 1932, when I was disallowed because I had not qualified for the necessary contributory period of thirty weeks. After this I was given a food ticket for 23s. a week, which continued until January, 1933, when it was stopped because of the Means Test. Before the stoppage our income was over the minimum limit of £2 17s. 6d. So now we have to depend on the boys and they have to keep all six of us, including my wife and the two children who are still going to school . . .

'What effect has unemployment had on me? It has definitely lessened my interest in politics, because it has led me to believe that politics is a game of bluff, and that these people do not care a brass farthing for the bottom dog . . . the same applies to the trade unions; when it comes to the real test they are hopeless.'

*H. L. Beales and R. S. Lambert, 'Memoirs of the Unemployed',
1934*

The Nation's Health, 1918–39

Medical Progress in the Inter-War Years.
Edward Mellanby, Recent Advances in Medical Science
(*Cambridge*, *1939*), pp. *11–18*.

ADVANCES IN THE CONTROL
OF HUMAN DISEASE

While the physiologist and pathologist have been patiently
building up the foundation of knowledge of the body in
health and disease and providing the basis upon which all
advancement in medical science depends, others have investigated the more applied side of curative and preventive
medicine. The immunologist has taught mankind how to
control, either by prevention or cure, many infective diseases
by inoculation with toxins, toxoids and antitoxins, vaccines
and antisera. Increased control has thus been obtained over
diphtheria, measles, whooping cough, cerebrospinal fever,
tetanus and anthrax. The extension of physiology and bio-
chemistry, even in the last twenty-five years, has opened up the
field of nutritional disease and thereby provided control of
such conditions as rickets, osteomalacia, defective tooth for-
mation, scurvy, beri-beri, pellagra and night blindness, and
also revolutionised the most important subject of feeding,
especially of infants and growing children.

Since antipyrin, acetanilide and phenacetin were prepared
in the laboratory and prescribed for the relief of pain fifty
years ago, the use of synthetic drugs for the treatment of
symptoms and indeed for the actual cure of disease has
achieved great success. The introduction of organic arsenicals
by Ehrlich in 1910 for the cure of syphilis was followed by
the discovery of other synthetic drugs for the cure of malaria,
bilharzia, kala azar and sleeping sickness. In the past three
years we have seen the wonderful effects of another type of
chemotherapeutic agent, namely, the sulphanilamide de-
rivatives which, from the point of view of disease in this
country, probably represent the greatest advance in treatment of the present century. Until these discoveries were
made, no instance of chemotherapeutic agent having a
specific effect on bacterial infections was known. Now

streptococcal meningococcal and pneumococcal infections, previously the most deadly of all diseases, have for the most part been brought under control. Sepsis and septicaemia of childbirth, meningitis, erysipelas, gonorrhoea and infections of the genito-urinary tract and pneumonia are now treated successfully with such drugs as prontosil, sulphanilamide and the more recently discovered 2-sulphanilyl-aminopyridine. In the past month it was reported that, in a series of between 600 and 700 cases of pneumonia at Birmingham, the mortality rate was lowered, in the case of patients under fifty years of age, from 17 to 1·6 per cent and in patients over fifty years, from 50 to 24 per cent by the use of 2-sulphanilyl-aminopyridine (W. F. Gaisford, *Lancet*, 1939, I, 823). In observations made in the Sudan, the mortality rate of cerebrospinal fever was reduced from one varying between 70 and 95 per cent to 5 per cent by the use of these drugs.

Before leaving this subject of disease control, it is also necessary to refer in passing to the triumphs of recent work on hormones—to the modern methods of treating diabetes mellitus with insulin, pernicious anaemia with liver active principle, Addison's disease with substances prepared from the adrenal cortex, myxoedema with thyroxine, and various conditions amenable to treatment by sex hormones. This is also one of the most active divisions of medical science.

For brevity's sake it is only possible to recount here a few of the triumphs of modern medical research. These are the fruits of the tree, the tree itself being, from a scientific point of view, vastly more important than its fruit. May I also add that in this amazing growth there are no more active branches in the world than are found in the medical school of this university?

As for other outstanding examples of the effects on health and disease in man of the application of increments of knowledge, these can be cited briefly. The adoption of better standards of sanitation and cleanliness, developed and supported by the science of bacteriology and immunology, cleared out of the country many of the decimating diseases of past centuries. Plague, malaria, typhus, cholera and smallpox, which killed their thousands and tens of thousands, disappeared in the nineteenth century. Typhoid fever which, even in the year 1900 killed over 5000 people in this country, was responsible for the death of only 206 people in 1937, and any mild epidemic nowadays is liable to create a great public scandal.

Other infectious diseases, although still with us, have been reduced greatly in their killing power. Tuberculosis, which in the years 1871–80 killed annually in this country 2880 out of every 100,000 people, had a mortality rate of 690 only in 1937. Mortality due to scarlet fever sank from 720 per 100,000 people in the years 1871–80 to 9 in 1937. The corresponding figures for measles were 380 in 1871–80 and 26 in 1937; for whooping cough 510 in 1871–80 and 43 in 1937. These are some of the main fatal diseases in childhood, and it is on human life at this age that medical science has had its greatest influence.

Infant mortality has fallen in the last forty years from 156 per 1000 to 53 per 1000, but the corresponding figure of 31 per 1000 for New Zealand still indicates plenty of room for improvement. How great has been the change in childhood and early adult life can be understood from the fact that, whereas even so short a time ago as 1922, 42·5 per cent of all deaths in Britain occurred before the age of fifty, and 57·5 per cent after fifty, in 1937 only 27 per cent of deaths occurred under fifty and 73 per cent after this age.

With the shrinkage of the death-rate in early life, the rapid raising of the average age of the population and the postponement of death, there has been, as might be expected, an increased incidence in the fatal diseases of later life and probably an increase in the disabling and degenerative diseases associated with advancing years. As regards the former, the increase in mortality due to diseases of the heart and circulation has been exceptionally great in the present century. In 1935 the mortality rate due to heart disease was more than five times greater in this country than in 1921. As regards death due to angina pectoris, there was an increase amounting to 176 per cent in males and 206 per cent in females over the corresponding figures even such a short time ago as 1928. Apart from any differences in these figures that may be accounted for by differences of diagnosis or in age distribution, there is a strong suggestion that some harmful cause of heart disease and especially of coronary occlusion, probably some mistake in mode of living, has recently appeared in our midst or has become accentuated. This matter urgently needs attention by scientists.

As might be expected, deaths due to cancer have risen in recent years, the crude mortality rate having increased from 1336 per million living in 1925 to 1633 in 1937. Taking the crude mortality rate at 100 in 1901-10, the corresponding figure in 1935 was 204 among males and 155 among females. In view of the great difference in age distribution between these years, the increase is not surprising, and there is not much support for the view that cancer has increased more rapidly than can be accounted for by the large number of older people now living.

Were the effects of eliminating the mortal diseases of early life, which thereby postpone death, the only claims of medical science, they would be sufficiently large. But much more than this can be claimed for it. Almost as important is its effect on the quality of life and the general advance in physique and health of the population. Especially can this be seen in the physique of school boys and girls. In the twenty years, 1911-31, the average height and weight of boys of twelve years of age attending elementary schools in Leeds increased from 4 ft. 4 in. and 63·5 lb. to 4 ft. 7 in. and 74·4 lb. respectively. Sir Henry Bashford reports similar changes among those employed at the Post Office, the present-day boys aged sixteen being 16 lb. heavier and $1\frac{1}{2}$ in. taller than boys of the same age twenty-five years ago: girls of sixteen are 10 lb. heavier on an average and 1 in. taller than girls of the same age of the last generation. Most or all of these improvements in physique are now known to be due to changes in food habits, and to the increased consumption of the protective foods—milk, butter, eggs, fruit and vegetables—at the expense of bread and other cereals.

In addition to the improved height and weight, there has also been a great decrease in bone deformity in young people. Bandy legs in children, which used to be a matter of indifference or amusement, are now rare and their occurrence gives rise to feelings of indignation. Even in north-country towns, where rickets used to be a veritable plague, the reduction in its incidence has been very great, and cases are often difficult to find for teaching purposes. The decrease in bone and glandular tuberculosis has also been remarkable.

Probably sufficient has been said to indicate the nature and degree of decrease in disease and the improvement in health and physique made possible by the application of medical science in recent years.

Leisure 1918–39

The early days of cinema-going
J. B. Priestley, Angel Pavement (*London, 1930), pp. 174–6. Quoted in R. W. Breach and R. M. Hartwell,* British Economy and Society, 1870–1970 (*Oxford, 1972), pp. 151–4.*

At last the waitress came. She was a girl with a nose so long and so thickly powdered that a great deal of it looked as if it did not belong to her, and she was tired, exasperated, and ready at any moment to be snappy. She took the order—and it was for plaice and chips, tea, bread and butter, and cakes: the great tea of the whole fortnight—without any enthusiasm, but she returned in time to prevent Turgis from losing any more temper. For the next twenty minutes, happily engaged in grappling with this feast, he forgot all about girls, and when the food was done and he was lingering over his third cup of tea and a cigarette, though no possible girls came within sight, he felt dreamily content. His mind swayed vaguely to the tune the orchestra was playing. Adventure would come; and for the moment he was at ease, lingering on its threshold.

From this tropical plateau of tea and cakes, he descended into the street, where the harsh night air suddenly smote him. The pavements were all eyes and thick jostling bodies; at every corner, the newspaper sellers cried out their football editions in wailing voices of the doomed; cars went grinding and snarling and roaring past; and the illuminated signs glittered and rocketed beneath the forgotten faded stars. He arrived at his second destination, the Sovereign Picture Theatre, which towered at the corner like a vast spangled wedding-cake in stone. It might have been a twin of that great teashop he had just left; and indeed it was; another frontier outpost of the new age. Two Jews, born in Poland but now American citizens, had talked over cigars and coffee on the loggia of a crazy Spanish-Italian–American villa, within sight of the Pacific, and out of that talk (a very quiet talk, for one of the two men was in considerable pain and knew that he was dying inch by inch) there had sprouted this monster, together with other monsters that had suddenly appeared in New York, Paris, and Berlin. Across ten thousand miles, those two men had seen the one-and-sixpence in Turgis's pocket and, with a swift gesture, resolving itself magically into steel and concrete and carpets and velvet-covered seats and pay-boxes, had set it in motion and diverted it to themselves.

He waited now to pay his one-and-sixpence, standing in the queue at the Balcony entrance. It was only a little after six and the Saturday night rush had hardly begun, but soon there were at least a hundred of them standing there. Near Turgis, on either side, the sexes were neatly paired off. There were one or two middle-aged women but no unaccompanied girl in sight in the whole queue. The evening was not beginning too well.

When at last they were admitted, they first walked through an enormous entrance hall, richly tricked out in chocolate and gold, illuminated by a huge central candelabra, a vast bunch of russet gold globes. Footmen in chocolate and gold waved them towards the two great marble balustrades, the wide staircase lit with more russet gold globes, the prodigiously thick and opulent chocolate carpets, into which their feet sank as if they were the feet of archdukes and duchesses. Up they went, passing a chocolate and gold platoon or two and a portrait gallery of film stars, whose eyelashes seemed to stand out from the walls like stout black wires, until they reached a door that led them to the dim summit of the Balcony, which fell dizzily away in a scree of little heads. It was an interval between pictures. Several searchlights were focussed on an organ-keyboard that looked like a tiny gilded box, far below, and the organ itself was shaking out cascades of treacly sound, so that the whole place trembled with sugary ecstasies. But while they waited in the gangway, the lights faded out, the gilded box dimmed and sank, the curtains parted to reveal the screen again, and an enormous voice, as inhuman as that of a genie, announced that it would bring the world's news not only to their eyes but to their ears.

The Middle Classes, 1918–39

Changes in class characteristics in British Society.
George Orwell, The Lion and the Unicorn (London, 1941), pp.
50–5, quoted in R. W. Breach and R. M. Hartwell, British
Economy and Society, 1870–1970 *(Oxford, 1972), pp. 176–9.*

One of the most important developments in England during the past twenty years has been the upward and downward extension of the middle class. It has happened on such a scale as to make the old classification of society into capitalists, proletarians and petit-bourgeois (small property-owners) almost obsolete.

England is a country in which property and financial power are concentrated in very few hands. Few people in modern England *own* anything at all, except clothes, furniture and possibly a house. The peasantry have long since disappeared, the independent shopkeeper is being destroyed, the small businessman is diminishing in numbers. But at the same time modern industry is so complicated that it cannot get along without great numbers of managers, salesmen, engineers, chemists and technicians of all kinds, drawing fairly large salaries. And these in turn call into being a professional class of doctors, lawyers, teachers, artists, etc., etc. The tendency of advanced captalism has therefore been to enlarge the middle class and not to wipe it out as it once seemed likely to do.

But much more important than this is the spread of middle-class ideas and habits among the working class. The British working class are now better off in almost all ways than they were thirty years ago. This is partly due to the efforts of the Trade Unions, but partly to the mere advance of physical science. It is not always realized that within rather narrow limits the standard of life of a country can rise without a corresponding rise in real-wages. Up to a point, civilization can lift itself up by its boot-tags. However unjustly society is organized, certain technical advances are bound to benefit the whole community, because certain kinds of goods are necessarily held in common. A millionaire cannot, for example, light the streets for himself while darkening them for other people. Nearly all citizens of civilized countries now enjoy the use of good roads, germ-free water, police protection, free libraries and probably free education of a kind. Public education in England has been meanly starved of money, but it has nevertheless improved, largely owing to the devoted efforts of the teachers, and the habit of reading has become enormously more widespread. To an increasing extent the rich and the poor read the same books, and they also see the same films and listen to the same radio programmes. And the differences in their way of life have been diminished by the mass-production of cheap clothes and improvements in housing. So far as outward appearance goes, the clothes of rich and poor, especially in the case of women, differ far less than they did thirty or even fifteen years ago. As to housing, England still has slums which are a blot on civilization, but much building has been done during the past ten years, largely by the local authorities. The modern Council house, with its bathroom and electric light, is smaller than the stockbroker's villa, but it is recognizably the same kind of house, which the farm labourer's cottage is not. A person who has grown up in a Council housing estate is likely to be—indeed, visibly *is*—more middle class in outlook than a person who has grown up in a slum.

The effect of all this is a general softening of manners. It is enhanced by the fact that modern industrial methods tend always to demand less muscular effort and therefore to leave people with more energy when their day's work is done. Many workers in the light industries are less truly manual labourers than is a doctor or a grocer. In tastes, habits, manners and outlook the working class and the middle class are drawing together. The unjust distinctions remain, but the real differences diminish. The old-style 'proletarian'—collarless, unshaven and with muscles warped by heavy labour—still exists, but he is constantly decreasing in numbers; he only predominates in the heavy industry areas of the north of England.

After 1918 there began to appear something that had never existed in England before: people of indeterminate social class. In 1910 every human being in these islands could be 'placed' in an instant by his clothes, manners and accent. That is no longer the case. Above all, it is not the case in the new townships that have developed as a result of cheap motor cars and the southward shift of industry. The place to look for the germs of the future England is in the light-industry areas and along the arterial roads. In Slough, Dagenham, Barnet, Letchworth, Hayes—everywhere, indeed, on the outskirts of great towns—the old pattern is gradually changing into something new. In those vast new wildernesses of glass and brick the sharp distinctions of the older kind of town, with its slums and mansions, or of the country, with its manor-houses and squalid cottages, no longer exist. There are wider gradations of income, but it is the same kind of life that is being lived at different levels, in labour-saving flats or Council houses, along the concrete roads and in the naked democracy of the swimming pools. It is a rather restless, cultureless life, centring round tinned food, *Picture Post*, the radio and the internal combustion engine. It is a civilization in which children grow up with an intimate knowledge of magnetoes and in complete ignorance of the Bible. To that civilization belong the people who are most at home in and most definitely *of* the modern world, the technicians and the higher-paid skilled workers, the airmen and their mechanics, the radio experts, film producers, popular journalists and industrial chemists. They are the indeterminate stratum at which the older class distinctions are beginning to break down.

This war, unless we are defeated, will wipe out most of the existing class privileges. There are every day fewer people who wish them to continue. Nor need we fear that as the pattern changes life in England will lose its peculiar flavour. The new red cities of Greater London are crude enough, but these things are only the rash that accompanies a change. In whatever shape England emerges from the war, it will be deeply tinged with the characteristics that I have spoken of earlier. The intellectuals who hope to see it Russianized or Germanized will be disappointed. The gentleness, the hypocrisy, the thoughtlessness, the reverence for law and the hatred of uniforms will remain, along with the suet puddings and the misty skies.

Social Investigation, 1918–39.

Orwell mixed with the unemployed in his attempt to discover the condition of England in the 1930's. Here, he comments on the extent of poverty and the resources which were available to the unemployed.
George Orwell, The Road to Wigan Pier (*London, 1932*), *pp. 75–9.*

When you see the unemployment figures quoted at two millions, it is fatally easy to take this as meaning that two million people are out of work and the rest of the population is comparatively comfortable. I admit that till recently I was in the habit of doing so myself. I used to calculate that if you put the registered unemployed at round about two millions and threw in the destitute and those who for one reason and another were not registered, you might take the number of underfed people in England (for *everyone* on the dole or thereabouts is underfed) as being, at the very most, five millions.

This is an enormous under-estimate, because, in the first place, the only people shown on unemployment figures are those actually drawing the dole—that is, in general, heads of families. An unemployed man's dependants do not figure on the list unless they too are drawing a separate allowance. A Labour Exchange officer told me that to get the real number of people *living on* (not drawing) the dole, you have got to multiply the official figures by something over three. This alone brings the number of unemployed to round about six millions. But in addition there are great numbers of people who are in work but who, from a financial point of view, might equally well be unemployed, because they are not drawing anything that can be described as a living wage. Allow for these and their dependants, throw in as before the old-age pensioners, the destitute and other nondescripts, and you get an *underfed* population of well over ten millions. Sir John Orr puts it at twenty millions.

Take the figures for Wigan, which is typical enough of the industrial and mining districts. The number of insured workers is round about 36,000 (26,000 men and 10,000 women). Of these, the number unemployed at the beginning of 1936 was about 10,000. But this was in winter when the mines are working full time; in summer it would probably be 12,000. Multiply by three, as above, and you get 30,000 or 36,000. The total population of Wigan is a little under 87,000; so that at any moment more than one person in three out of the whole population—not merely the registered workers—is either drawing or living on the dole. Those ten or twelve thousand unemployed contain a steady core of from four to five thousand miners who have been continuously unemployed for the past seven years. And Wigan is not especially badly off as industrial towns go. Even in Sheffield, which has been doing well for the last year or so because of wars and rumours of war, the proportion of unemployment is about the same—one in three of registered workers unemployed.

When a man is first unemployed, until his insurance stamps are exhausted, he draws "full benefit," of which the rates are as follows:

	per week
Single man	17s.
Wife	9s.
Each child below 14 . . .	3s.

Thus in a typical family of parents and three children of whom one was over 14, the total income would be 32s. per week, plus anything that might be earned by the eldest child. When a man's stamps are exhausted, before being turned over to the P.A.C. (Public Assistance Committee), he receives twenty-six weeks' "transitional benefit" from the U.A.B. (Unemployment Assistance Board), the rates being as follows:

	per week
Single man	15s.
Man and wife	24s.
Children, 14–18	6s.
Children, 11–14	4s. 6d.
Children, 8–11	4s.
Children, 5–8	3s. 6d.
Children, 3–5	3s.

Thus on the U.A.B. the income of the typical family of five persons would be 37s. 6d. a week if no child was in work. When a man is on the U.A.B. a quarter of his dole is regarded as rent, with a minimum of 7s. 6d. a week. If the

rent he is paying is more than a quarter of his dole he receives
an extra allowance, but if it is less than 7s. 6d., a corresponding amount is deducted. Payments on the P.A.C. theoretically
come out of the local rates, but are backed by a central fund.
The rates of benefit are:

				per week
Single man	.	.	. .	12s. 6d.
Man and wife	.	.	.	23s.
Eldest child	.	.	.	4s.
Any other child	.	.	.	3s.

Being at the discretion of the local bodies these rates vary
slightly, and a single man may or may not get an extra 2s. 6d.
weekly, bringing his benefit up to 15s. As on the U.A.B., a
quarter of a married man's dole is regarded as rent. Thus in
the typical family considered above the total income would be
33s. a week, a quarter of this being regarded as rent. In
addition, in most districts a coal allowance of 1s. 6d. a week
(1s. 6d. is equivalent to about a hundredweight of coal) is
granted for six weeks before and six weeks after Christmas.

It will be seen that the income of a family on the dole
normally averages round about thirty shillings a week. One
can write at least a quarter of this off as rent, which is to say
that the average person, child or adult, has got to be fed,
clothed, warmed, and otherwise cared-for for six or seven
shillings a week. Enormous groups of people, probably at
least a third of the whole population of the industrial areas,
are living at this level. The Means Test is very strictly
enforced, and you are liable to be refused relief at the
slightest hint that you are getting money from another source.
Dock-labourers, for instance, who are generally hired by the
half day, have to sign on at a Labour Exchange twice daily; if
they fail to do so it is assumed that they have been working
and their dole is reduced correspondingly. I have seen cases
of evasion of the Means Test, but I should say that in the
industrial towns, where there is still a certain amount of
communal life and everyone has neighbours who know him,
it is much harder than it would be in London. The usual
method is for a young man who is actually living with his
parents to get an accommodation address, so that supposedly
he has a separate establishment and draws a separate allowance. But there is much spying and tale-bearing. One man I

knew, for instance, was seen feeding his neighbour's chickens while the neighbour was away. It was reported to the authorities that he "had a job feeding chickens" and he had great difficulty in refuting this. The favourite joke in Wigan was about a man who was refused relief on the ground that he "had a job carting firewood." He had been seen, it was said, carting firewood at night. He had to explain that he was not carting firewood but doing a moonlight flit. The "firewood" was his furniture.

The most cruel and evil effect of the Means Test is the way in which it breaks up families. Old people, sometimes bedridden, are driven out of their homes by it. An old age pensioner, for instance, if a widower, would normally live with one or other of his children; his weekly ten shillings goes towards the household expenses, and probably he is not badly cared for. Under the Means Test, however, he counts as a "lodger" and if he stays at home his children's dole will be docked. So, perhaps at seventy or seventy-five years of age, he has to turn out into lodgings, handing his pension over to the lodging-house keeper and existing on the verge of starvation. I have seen several cases of this myself. It is happening all over England at this moment, thanks to the Means Test.

Nevertheless, in spite of the frightful extent of unemployment, it is a fact that poverty—extreme poverty—is less in evidence in the industrial North than it is in London. Everything is poorer and shabbier, there are fewer motor-cars and fewer well-dressed people; but also there are fewer people who are obviously destitute. Even in a town the size of Liverpool or Manchester you are struck by the fewness of the beggars. London is a sort of whirlpool which draws derelict people towards it, and it is so vast that life there is solitary and anonymous. Until you break the law nobody will take any notice of you, and you can go to pieces as you could not possibly do in a place where you had neighbours who knew you.

Evacuees and the 'Blitz'

The development of military aircraft between 1919–39 had caused much worry to governments and defence chiefs. The effects of aerial bombing had been shown in a number of conflicts but especially during the Spanish Civil War (1936–9). It was a popular belief that in the first hours of a major conflict great air forces would attack enemy cities and reduce whole districts to rubble.

On 1st September 1939 more than 36 hours before Britain's declaration of war a 'blackout' was declared. Windows were to be covered with a dark-coloured blind or heavy shutters so that no lights could be seen by a passing aircraft. This cost some large factories several thousand pounds each. Street lights were switched off at night and motor vehicles were not allowed to use their headlights. This led to many amusing incidents but also to a doubling of the number of road deaths until 'masked' headlights were permitted. In February 1940 a 20 m.p.h. speed limit was introduced for night driving. The electric trolley-bus became known as the 'silent peril' because it gave no warning of its approach. The 'blackout' lasted until May 1945.

Since large cities were believed to be the main target it was

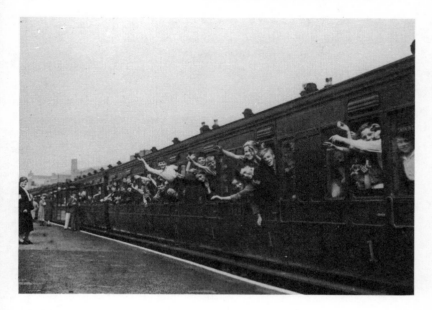

Evacuees leaving London, 1939

decided to evacuate to safer (country) areas all primary school children and their teachers and mothers with children under five years old. This was a total of four million persons but only about a third actually went. Some two million also went privately. The majority were carried by 4,000 special trains. Londoners went to East Anglia, Kent and the West. Liverpudlians were taken to North Wales and Glaswegians to the Lowlands of Scotland. Children from the other major cities were dispersed into the villages and small towns of the surrounding countryside.

The arrival of hundreds of thousands of city dwellers, many of them from poor, overcrowded homes, created many difficulties. Children got lost; they refused all food except fish and chips. They shocked their hosts by their unwillingness to wash or change their clothes. They found the quiet village life without cinemas, shops and other amusements boring.

Meanwhile the German bombers had failed to appear over Britain's cities and large numbers of evacuees drifted back to their original homes. By the end of 1939 nearly one million had done so. A new scheme was then drawn up which required parents to sign an agreement not to withdraw their children. By June 1942 the total number of persons who had moved home during the war—this included servicemen and war workers—was 20 million.

The evacuees from the major cities therefore, escaped the effects of the German air raids in 1940–1 and the 'flying bomb' attacks of 1944–5. The first attacks came in June 1940 and were intended to destroy the R.A.F. before a seaborne invasion was attempted. In September 1940, however, Hitler ordered his air force to begin bombing London and other major cities in retaliation for British bombing of German cities. Although the death and damage amongst the British was far less than that suffered in Germany, Japan, Poland and Russia, the total fatalities were more than 60,000. In addition 200,000 houses were destroyed and another 250,000 made uninhabitable. Since the amount of house-building which was possible during the war was only slight, Britain reached 1945 with a massive housing shortage.

To meet the bombing threat the Government had preparations other than simple evacuation. The R.A.F. Fighter Command trained in defensive fighting and forewarned by radar and the Royal

Bomb damage at Bank tube station

Observer Corps, was the first line of defence. This meant that much of the early fighting took place over Kent and Sussex. Anti-aircraft guns shot down some of the raiders that got through. Finally Air Raid Wardens sounded warning sirens and later an 'all clear' to the people in danger. When the 'alert' was sounded civilians hurried to the nearest shelter. Mostly these were 'oblong brick-built structures, with a flat concrete roof, resembling a garage'. They contained benches, a lavatory and electric lighting but, of course, no windows. Londoners soon began to use the platforms of underground railway stations. By September 1940 almost 180,000 persons a night were taking shelter there.

As early as 1938 the Home Secretary, Sir John Anderson, had ordered a design for a cheap air-raid shelter which could be installed in a garden. By late 1940 more than 2 million of these, each capable of holding about six people, had been made. The installation of an 'Anderson' shelter required a great deal of digging and because it was sunk to a depth of more than 1 metre it soon filled with water. Nevertheless it could resist the blast of a 45 kg bomb at a range of 2 metres. The other principal type of shelter, made completely of steel plates and heavy wire mesh, was installed into homes and looked rather like a table.

London was the principal target of the German air force, as Berlin was to become that of the R.A.F. Coventry, Hull and Liverpool suffered heavily but Sheffield escaped lightly. By mid-1941, after one massive raid which killed 1,436 Londoners in one night, the might of Germany was turned on Russia, and not until the development of V-rocket bombs in 1944 did aerial warfare become a serious threat once more to Britain.

War Workers and Industry

Britain entered the war with more than a million persons unemployed and by the time of the fall of France in June 1940 this figure had scarcely been reduced. This illustrates the casual way in which the Chamberlain government acted during its last months in office. New ministries had been set up in 1939 and early 1940. These were for Home Security, Economic Warfare, Information, Food, Shipping and Aircraft Production, but there was little confidence in the Government.

During the disastrous defeats in Scandinavia and France (April–May 1940), Winston Churchill became Prime Minister and set up an all-party government.

For Minister of Labour he chose Ernest Bevin, the greatest trade union leader of the time. With the realisation that Britain was now alone and even threatened with invasion but with a government they could trust, Britain's workers and union leaders co-operated fully in the war effort.

To continue the struggle Britain had to boost production in two sectors—munitions and agriculture—whilst allowing most others, especially 'luxury' items, to be run down. Since Britain bought a great deal of food from abroad valuable space aboard ships could be saved by 'ploughing up'. The amount of land growing cereal crops was increased by 50 per cent during the war. County War Agricultural Committees were set up with great power to decide on how land should be used and where workers, machinery and fertilisers should be employed. Inefficient farmers could be made to give up their land. The extra workers needed were supplied by the newly-formed Women's Land Army, by those who refused to join the armed forces for reasons of conscience and later by German and Italian prisoners. Between 1939 and 1943 corn crop production increased 260 per cent[1] and milk production also rose but meat products fell by 30 per cent, the obvious result of ploughing up pasture.

The munitions industry depended basically upon steel and chemical products. The Government exercised control in this field by making itself solely responsible for the allocation of raw materials. Additionally, very heavy taxes (purchase tax) were placed on luxury items. This meant that certain industries such as aircraft and vehicle production expanded rapidly whilst others such as furniture-making contracted. Workers moved out the latter into the former. Ernest Bevin, as Minister of Labour, was given very wide powers by Parliament to direct men to particular jobs and also to order particular conditions of work. Late in 1941 Bevin was enabled to conscript women between 20 and 30 years; in 1943 the age bracket was extended to include those from $18\frac{1}{2}$–50 years.

The work force increased by six million over the 1939 number, with a large growth in trade union membership. The shortage of coal, partly as a result of miners joining the forces, resulted in 22,000 men being ordered to work in coal mines. They became known as 'Bevin boys'.

By mid-1943 there were 24 million persons employed in the armed forces and industry. Of these eight million were women and one million old age pensioners. Women made up between a third and two-fifths of the labour force in aircraft production and engineering and a *majority* of the work force in ammunition and explosives factories. Domestic service almost disappeared as a paid job. Many thousands of young women had to leave home and take lodgings in order to work at an aircraft or munitions factory. Frequently this meant rising at 6 a.m. to catch special transport to work and after an 11-hour day returning exhausted in the evening. As in the First

[1] The harvests of 1942 and 1943 were each successively 'the best on record'.

World War women were also employed on trams, buses and railway trains, as well as in more unusual occupations such as crane-driving and telephone engineering.

The co-operation of the trade unions with the Government and the setting up of various wages councils prevented serious inflation. As a result of pay increases and longer hours wages rose more quickly than the cost of living. Weekly earnings were 80 per cent higher in 1945 than they had been in 1938, whilst the cost of living rose by only 30 per cent during the war period. Income tax reached 10s (50p) in the pound but the shortage of goods and rationing meant that most spare money went into savings which helped the war effort.

Rationing

As the war progressed increasing numbers of workers and factory plant were turned over to the war effort and 'luxury' imports were reduced. So it became necessary to ration food and other commodities to prevent massive price increases and to ensure a fair distribution. The Government was slow to start rationing until it discovered that the public actually wanted it.

In January 1940 bacon, sugar and butter were restricted to a few ounces per week for each person. Meat, tea and fats were also added to the list of rationed goods in 1940. Various other items such as jam were included in 1941 but bread, sausages and, if it could be found, fish remained unrationed throughout the war.

In December 1941 some foods began to be listed on a 'points' system by the Ministry of Food and each person was given 16 (and later 20) points per month to spend as he wished. To prevent a 'run' on popular foods the points value was increased and that of unpopular foods reduced. Whalemeat appeared in fishmongers' shops but was regarded with distaste by most people. So also were American dried eggs in powder form, brought in to replace the shortage of home-produced eggs. Dried milk powder was another wartime development.

To ensure that children did not go hungry the school meals system was vastly extended until it provided for 2 million pupils

Food rationing begins, January 1940

per day. Ice-cream, however, disappeared between 1942 and 1945. Most factories set up cheap canteens and the public could make use of one of the 2,000 British Restaurants which provided a cooked meal for about 1s (5p). At first those with sufficient money could eat well at expensive restaurants and hotels. The Government then made it illegal to serve more than one main course per meal and in June 1942 the maximum price for a meal was fixed at 5s (25p). To prevent a rapid rise in food prices it was still found necessary for the Government to pay 'subsidies' to farmers and importers. By 1945 £250 million of taxation was being channelled back through food subsidies. The shortage of petrol caused by the torpedo attacks on tankers and the enormous demands of the bomber forces, led to the abolition of all private motoring throughout the last three years of the war. Petrol rationing had begun on 22nd September 1939, providing enough fuel for about 60 or 70 kilometres a week. Despite efforts by drivers to economise by free-wheeling the ration was steadily reduced.

By 1944 only 700,000 'essential' private cars were left on the roads, one-third of the 1939 figure. The manufacture of private cars ceased between 1940 and 1945 but petrol rationing continued until 1950. Britain's mainly steam-hauled railways were called upon to carry 50 per cent more freight by 1944 than in 1938 and over 75 per cent more passengers.

Clothes rationing was introduced in June 1941 and as a result spending on clothing fell to less than half the pre-war rate. The main purpose of this scheme was to allow almost half a million clothing workers and their factories to be used for the war effort. Whereas men did not mind too much having to walk around in shabby clothes, women did. Old clothes had to be patched up and new ones made from curtaining, bed-linen and even parachute material.

Cigarettes were not rationed during the war and valuable space was taken up in ships and valuable dollars spent bringing tobacco to Britain. Under the strain of wartime conditions many people, especially women, took up smoking for the first time. By early 1941 cigarettes had become scarce and soon thousands of people were walking from shop to shop in search of a 'packet of ten'. If refused by the shopkeeper some people became abusive and angry; others tried bribery. Some smokers gained extra value by putting cigarette butts into a pipe, others were forced to try strange brands such as Turkish Pashas which appeared on the market. Similarly, alcoholic drinks became scarce. With the war in Europe cutting off supplies of French and Italian wines and whisky production down by two-thirds, the cost of drinking rose rapidly. By 1941 beer was also in short supply. Pubs opened late or not at all on some nights and customers were 'rationed'. The drinks situation was made worse by a chronic shortage of bottles. There was no coal rationing during the war, despite careful plans which had been drawn up for this. Instead the Ministry of Fuel and Power urged everyone to economise. Additionally, thousands of miners who had joined up were released from the forces and other young men were directed, most unwillingly, to collieries instead of to army camps.

Nevertheless, coal remained in short supply throughout the war and in cold weather families took to wearing overcoats indoors. Timber from bombed houses was soon taken for fuel, as were whole trees in more isolated areas.

Two forms of entertainment which continued throughout the war were the cinema and horse-racing, although both the Football League and County Cricket Championship competitions were suspended. Cinemas were usually crowded (which meant long queues) and remained so even during air raids. Besides offering entertainment they could be used to give information and advice helpful to the war effort.

Welfare Services

The great upheavals in British society during the Second World War soon showed up the gaps in the welfare services. Evacuee children needed meals and medical attention as also did war victims and munitions workers injured or exhausted from long hours of work. Old age pensioners needed extra money to pay for higher-priced goods. Victims of air raids needed shelter, clothing and food. As the war progressed and rationing, blackouts and bomb-shelters came to be shared by all, two factors clearly emerged. First, that the welfare services, as they had been built up piecemeal before 1939, were in a chaotic condition. Secondly, that if everyone had a right to share in both the dangers and the comforts of wartime, so also had they a right to a share of the peace. The Second World War helped enormously in breaking up the selective welfare system and thereby paving the way for the universal and comprehensive post-war system.

As early as June 1941 the coalition government set up a committee to investigate the existing schemes of social insurance and make recommendations. Sir William Beveridge, a distinguished scholar and civil servant, was chosen to be chairman of this commit-

Sir William Beveridge—
the main architect of the
Welfare State

tee which published its long report in November 1942. The report entitled *Social Insurance and Allied Services* was soon selling by the hundred thousand and was translated into many languages, including Chinese.

The Beveridge Report dealt with the major social evil of poverty or want. The other great social evils were so immense that they would require special attention from particular government departments. *Disease* would be tackled by a full-scale National Health Service; *squalor* through the building of new homes; *idleness* through the expansion of new jobs and *ignorance* through the expansion of education. Poverty has many causes and Beveridge proposed benefits and allowances designed to rescue all unfortunate enough to be in serious need. These allowances included unemployment benefit, dependants' pensions, maternity benefits and family allowances. 'National Assistance' was also proposed to provide for those who slipped through the net or were somehow left with insufficient benefits for their needs.

To organise such a massive scheme in which *every* citizen would be included, Beveridge proposed a single Ministry of Social Security. It would handle payments and collect weekly flat-rate contributions in the form of a single stamp on a single card which would be paid for jointly by both employer and employee. Adequate flat-rate benefits were to be paid for an unlimited period if necessary. It was proposed that the Treasury would pay 50 per cent of the cost, the workers 30 per cent and the employers 20 per cent.

Beveridge's suggestions were received with great enthusiasm in Britain with the unhappy memories of the 1930's still strong. The Government, totally involved in the war effort, could not make firm commitments particularly since there had been no General Election since 1935. However, the House of Commons voted nearly three to one in favour of the report. The Prime Minister, Winston Churchill, in a broadcast in March 1943, made no direct promises but had to admit that a period of major reconstruction was necessary after the war.

In two other fields the wartime government acted more swiftly. First, in the field of education the war had shown up many shortcomings. In 1944 Mr. R. A. Butler, the Education Minister, laid a bill before Parliament to provide free secondary education for all. Education was to be reorganised into primary, secondary and further spheres. (This Act was for England and Wales only.)

The school-leaving age was to be raised to 15 as soon as possible (but in fact delayed until 1947) and 16 soon after (but actually took place in 1972). At 11 years of age children would sit an examination and would then go to a grammar, technical or modern school. The 1944 Act also planned a considerable expansion of higher education with 'grants' for needy students.

In 1943 the Government also set up a new Ministry, of Town and Country Planning. Very few new houses were built during the war (9,000 in 1943) but in March 1945 a target of 300,000 per year was set. To overcome the immediate shortage, it was also planned to spend £150 million on 'pre-fab' houses small and quickly assembled prefabricated units made of corrugated iron and asbestos.

The Economy in 1945

Britain was at war for slightly over 2,000 days and the cost rose from £1 million *per day* to an enormous £16 million *per day* by 1945. This heavy burden was met by five major means. First, income tax was raised to 10s (50p) in the pound and firms were similarly affected, particularly if they were supplying war materials and thereby doing more business. Excess profits tax was levied. Second, people were encouraged to save through Government loans, partly through patriotism, partly because consumer goods (cars, furniture etc.,) were almost impossible to obtain. Third, some of Britain's overseas investments, totalling £1,200 million (25 per cent of the total) were sold off. Fourth, Britain obtained large amounts of goods on credit from abroad totalling £3,500 million. Fifth, Britain received free gifts of money and materials from Canada and the U.S.A. totalling £7,500 million. U.S. aid was known as 'lend-lease'.

It was obvious as early as 1940 that Britain did not have the economic strength to fight the war single-handed. Without the huge contributions of the U.S.A. and the Commonwealth and Empire, Britain would have been unable to continue. However, from 1940–4

Britain was the only major area in Western Europe from which Germany could be attacked. The American and Commonwealth leaders realised that Britain, and from 1941 the U.S.S.R., *had* to be helped on a large scale if Europe were to be freed from the Nazis. The help which the U.S.A. in particular gave through 'lend-lease' was therefore not simply a 'free gift' to Britain, but a vital part of winning the war for the United Nations.

Britain ended the war as one of the victorious 'Big Three'. Whilst she had not spilt as much blood as Russia or spent as much as America, the war had cost Britain heavily. The death roll was nearly 400,000. Over 11 million tonnes of shipping had been lost and 500,000 houses destroyed or seriously damaged. The total shortage of houses was officially estimated at 1·25 million. The railways had been heavily overworked and under-maintained. Locomotives and rolling stock were in a seriously run-down condition. Similarly, many factories and their plant and equipment had been allowed to deteriorate seriously in an effort to squeeze the most out of them. The same situation applied to the coal mines but in their case production had *fallen*, from 227 million tonnes in 1937 to 182 million in 1945. The 'balance of payments' situation was critical. In simple terms Britain was spending far more abroad, mainly on the war effort, than she was earning. Exports had fallen 60 per cent and a deficit of £750 million was forecast for 1946. Additionally, the Americans announced within one week of Japan's surrender (August 1945) that 'lend-lease' was being stopped. Since the rest of the world was also largely disrupted by the war Britain's only solution appeared to lie in more massive American aid. This was negotiated in the form of a $4,400 million loan with an extra $1,250 million from Canada, all repayable over 50 years from 1951 at an interest rate of 2 per cent. Britain's only hope lay in quickly returning to peacetime production and supplying to the world the machines, ships, vehicles, chemicals and electrical goods which were needed in large quantities.

Document

War, 1939–45

Churchill's fighting speech of defiance, 4th June 1940, informing the world that in spite of early defeats "We shall go on to the end".
W. S. Churchill, Into Battle (*London, 1941*), *pp. 221–3.*

We are told that Herr Hitler has a plan for invading the British Isles. This has often been thought of before. When Napoleon lay at Boulogne for a year with his flat-bottomed boats and his Grand Army, he was told by someone "There are bitter weeds in England." There are certainly a great many more of them since the British Expeditionary Force returned.

The whole question of home defence against invasion is, of course, powerfully affected by the fact that we have for the time being in this island incomparably more powerful military forces than we have ever had at any moment in this war or the last. But this will not continue. We shall not be content with a defensive war. We have our duty to our Ally. We have to reconstitute and build up the British Expeditionary Force once again, under its gallant Commander-in-Chief, Lord Gort. All this is in train; but in the interval we must put our defences in this island into such a high state of organisation that the fewest possible numbers will be required to give effective security and that the largest possible potential of offensive effort may be realised. On this we are now engaged. . . .

We have found it necessary to take measures of increasing stringency, not only against enemy aliens and suspicious characters of other nationalities, but also against British subjects who may become a danger or a nuisance should the war be transported to the United Kingdom. I know there are a great many people affected by the orders which we have made who are the passionate enemies of Nazi Germany. I am very sorry for them, but we cannot, at the present time and under the present stress, draw all the distinctions which we should like to do. If parachute landings were attempted and fierce fighting attendant upon them followed, these unfortunate people would be far better out of the way, for their own sakes as well as for ours. There is, however, another class, for which I feel not the slightest sympathy. Parliament has given us the powers to put down Fifth Column activities with a strong hand, and we shall use those powers, subject to the supervision and correction of the House, without the slightest hesitation until we are satisfied, and more than satisfied, that this malignancy in our midst has been effectively stamped out.

Turning once again, and this time more generally, to the question of invasion, I would observe that there has never been a period in all these long centuries of which we boast when an absolute guarantee against invasion, still less against serious raids, could have been given to our people. In the days of Napoleon the same wind which would have carried his transports across the Channel might have driven away the blockading fleet. There was always the chance, and it is that chance which has excited and befooled the imaginations of many Continental tyrants. Many are the tales that are told. We are assured that novel methods will be adopted, and when we see the originality of malice, the ingenuity of aggression, which our enemy displays, we may certainly prepare ourselves for every kind of novel strategem and every kind of brutal and treacherous manoeuvre. I think that no idea is so outlandish that it should not be considered and viewed with a searching, but at the same time, I hope, with a steady eye. We must never forget the solid assurances of sea-power and those which belong to air power if it can be locally exercised.

I have, myself, full confidence that if all do their duty, if nothing is neglected, and if the best arrangements are made, as they are being made, we shall prove ourselves once again able to defend our island home, to ride out the storm of war, and to outlive the menace of tyranny, if necessary for years, if necessary alone. At any rate, that is what we are going to try to do. That is the resolve of His Majesty's Government— every man of them. That is the will of Parliament and the nation. The British Empire and the French Republic, linked together in their cause and in their need, will defend to the death their native soil, aiding each other like good comrades to the utmost of their strength. Even though large tracts of Europe and many old and famous States have fallen or may fall into the grip of the Gestapo and all the odious apparatus of Nazi rule, we shall not flag or fail. We shall go on to the end, we shall fight in France, we shall fight on the seas and oceans, we shall fight with growing confidence and growing strength in the air, we shall defend our island, whatever the cost may be, we shall fight on the beaches, we shall fight on the landing grounds, we shall fight in the fields and in the streets, we shall fight in the hills; we shall never surrender, and even if, which I do not for a moment believe, this island or a large part of it were subjugated and starving, then our Empire beyond the seas, armed and guarded by the British Fleet, would carry on the struggle, until, in God's good time, the new world, with all its power and might, steps forth to the rescue and the liberation of the old.

The Industrial Worker

British industry enjoyed many advantages for the first few years of peace. Most of her major competitors, Belgium, France, Germany, Italy, Japan and Poland were painfully rebuilding their ruined cities. Few countries had dollars to spare for American goods. In Britain, following the smooth change-over from wartime to peacetime production exports rose from £917 million worth in 1946 to £2,585 million by 1951. Imports, particularly of engineering products, rose even faster as industry and transport rebuilt and re-equipped itself.

Coal was still much the most important source of energy in Britain after 1945. Not only did coal supply the booming steel and manufacturing industries but also gas works and electricity power stations, the steam-hauled railways and domestic consumers. The coal industry had suffered serious problems during the war and by 1945 production had slumped to 180 million tonnes (where it had been 240 million tonnes in 1937). In 1947 coal was nationalised at a cost of £166 million making the state the owner of more than 900 collieries and the employer of 700,000 miners. With the large demand for coal, production was increased, passing 200 million tonnes per annum in 1950. It remained above this level until 1958, whilst the labour force fell only slightly. The new National Coal Board began to spend large amounts of money modernising the more profitable collieries. This took a long time to produce results and productivity (output per man) rose only 16 per cent over the first ten years of nationalisation. Safety standards improved more quickly with the number of deaths underground falling from 584 in 1947 to fewer than 300 in 1960, and fewer than 100 in 1969. The earnings of coalminers rose more quickly than the national average during the 1950's but after 1960 the industry began to run into difficulties. Coal began to be replaced by oil, electricity (including nuclear power) and natural gas from the North Sea. Even though productivity increased by more than one-third during the 1960's hundreds of collieries, particularly in Scotland, South Wales and north-east England, were closed.

By 1971 the number of coalminers in Britain had fallen to fewer than 300,000. Wages had failed to keep up and after some local strikes, the National Union of Mineworkers declared a national strike, the first since 1926. During the early weeks of 1972 the electricity power stations, deprived of fuel, began cutting off supplies and disrupting industry. In contrast to the events of 1926, the miners emerged victorious and gained a pay increase of between 30 and 40 per cent.

The production of steel, upon which so much of modern industry depends, also rose quickly from 12 million tonnes in 1945 and reached 16·3 million tonnes by 1950. The Labour government (1945–51) began nationalising the steel industry towards the end of its term of office and the incoming Conservatives (1951–64) were able to de-nationalise it in 1953. This situation was reversed once more in 1967 by the Labour government (1964–70) and from amongst the major firms in Britain the British Steel Corporation (B.S.C.) was born. Steel production continued to rise until it exceeded 27 million tonnes by 1970. The traditional steel producing areas such as the North East, Scotland, Sheffield and the West Midlands were rapidly outstripped by the newer 'coastal' works of South Wales and North Lincolnshire. By 1970 the B.S.C. was planning to shut down older less efficient works in Lancashire and Scotland and concentrate production in the newer areas. Whilst the total exports of finished steel rose from 1·3 million tonnes in 1948 to 3·6 million tonnes in 1968 this represented only about 12 per cent of total production. As more countries have begun to produce their own steel and competition from Japan and Germany has increased, the British steel industry has been unable to develop as quickly as other major industries and has had to suffer some serious financial losses.

One of the principal users of steel, the shipbuilding industry, has also suffered from international competition, again from Japan, which since 1956 has dominated the production of tankers and other bulk carriers. In 1945 there was a serious shortage of shipping and despite the lack of modern equipment British yards gained plenty of orders.

In 1948 a labour force of 255,000 men launched 332 new vessels of almost 1 million tonnes gross weight. By 1970 investments in new equipment enabled a labour force reduced to less than 200,000 to produce 180 new vessels of 1·3 million tonnes gross weight. Thus fewer and larger ships were being produced but Britain's total share in the world market had rapidly fallen. Only massive Government subsidies prevented wholesale bankruptcies amongst British ship producers but even these could not prevent very high unemployment in the shipbuilding areas of Clydeside, Merseyside, Belfast and the north-east coast.

By contrast motor vehicle production has risen steadily since 1945 (apart from slight falls in certain years of the 1960's). The production of motor cars everywhere had almost ceased (except of large expensive American vehicles) between 1939 and 1945. World demand for cars was, therefore, enormous and until the early 1950's British makers were almost without challenge. In 1950 nearly 66 per cent of British output was exported. Home demand was kept down

Silent shipyards

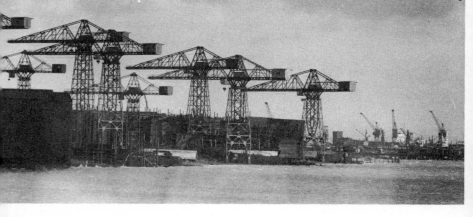

by a heavy purchase tax. Production of new cars first exceeded 500,000 in 1950 and one million by 1958 but had not reached two million by the early 1970's by reason of increasing European and Japanese competition. Although new factories were established in Scotland and Liverpool most British cars were still being made in the West Midlands, Luton and Dagenham. This was one of the main reasons why wages and therefore, general prosperity continued to be much higher in southern Britain, a trend begun in the 1920's.

The development of road transport affected the railways much more seriously in the 1950's than it had in the 1930's. By 1956 British Railways (nationalised in 1947) began to run into debt and wholesale closures of unprofitable lines and stations began. By 1970 British Rail had only 11,800 miles (19,000 km) of track and 2,868 stations compared with 19,600 miles (32,000 km) and 7,762 stations in 1948. Sizeable towns such as Mansfield, St. Andrews and Caernarvon were left without passenger trains. Hundreds of thousands of railwaymen were retired early or dismissed. However, with the replacement of steam locomotives by diesels, the electrification of the route from London to Birmingham, Manchester and (by 1974) Glasgow, and even higher speeds promised from the Advanced Passenger Train, the future of British Rail, began to look better by the early 1970's than it had done before 1960.

Despite the rapid growth of air travel in the 1950's and 1960's (there was an increase from 586,000 passengers in 1947 to 13·8 million in 1970) the British aircraft industry has had to rely very heavily upon Government orders for military aircraft and other subsidised development. For example, between 1962–72 the British and French governments shared a bill of over £1,000 million to build Concorde. The basic trouble is that aircraft research and development costs have risen enormously since 1945 and to recover these costs large sales are needed. This means exports and competition from the Americans is very tough. Smaller firms such as Handley Page have been unable to survive; others survived only by merging into larger companies. By 1970 only the British Aircraft Corporation and Hawker Siddeley were substantial manufacturers. Rolls-Royce alone manufactured aero engines but following a disastrous American contract, was saved from bankruptcy in 1971 only by Government aid.

The most successful industries in terms of growth and profitability are still chemicals and electricals. Chemical production rose by 85 per cent between 1948 and 1956 and 76 per cent between 1957 and 1967 while electrical production rose by 63 per cent during the latter decade. Chemical workers in 1971 were the second highest paid workers amongst major industrial groups whilst unemployment among them in 1971, when the U.K. total exceeded 900,000 (4 per cent), was less than 2 per cent. The electrical industry in Britain employed more than 900,000 workers in 1971 and although earnings were not quite as high as in chemicals unemployment was also extremely low.

The threat of unemployment which seemed to have disappeared during the post-war industrial boom began to return in the mid 1950's.

High employment has usually meant that earnings increase rapidly, since employers do not want to lose their workers. This was the case after 1945. Between 1947 and 1970 the average wage amongst industrial workers rose by 300 per cent whilst retail prices rose by only 250 per cent. This eventually meant that employers found that they had the choice of either losing increasing amounts of money or reducing the number of their workers. Most chose the latter course. For ten years the groups most affected were the same as in the 1920's and 1930's—coalminers, textile workers, shipbuilders, dockers, construction workers, especially after the 1966 'squeeze', and seasonal groups such as seaside workers. By 1970 even 'safe' industries such as motor vehicle manufacture, mechanical engineering and professional and scientific occupations were being seriously affected. By the end of 1971 some economists were suggesting that with the increased use of automatic machinery and computers in industry and government it was unlikely that unemployment would ever fall to the level of the immediate post-war period.

Town Life

As noted, Britain ended the Second World War as she had the First with a very serious housing shortage. The housing programme had received low priority with the result that only 3,095 units had been built during 1945. In addition, enemy action had destroyed or seriously damaged more than 400,000 dwellings. Many of these were very old but Britain still had hundreds of thousands of nineteenth-century slums to deal with also.

The immediate problem in 1945 was to provide accommodation quickly. One answer already mentioned, was prefabricated buildings. By the end of 1946 92,000 of these were erected. Meanwhile brick houses were also built—56,000 in 1946 and over 230,000 in 1948. By 1953 the figures had exceeded 300,000 but serious shortages remained, particularly in and around the major industrial cities.

To stem the spread of the great cities into the countryside around, 'green belts' have been set out. In addition a New Towns Act was passed in 1956.

This gave the Minister of Housing power to construct new towns several miles away to take the 'overspill' population. To accommodate Londoners ten new towns including Stevenage, Harlow and Crawley were set up. Glasgow's new towns are East Kilbride, Cumbernauld, Glenrothes, Irvine and Livingstone. Peterlee

A prefabricated house being put together, 1946

Factory-made houses

was set up in the North East, Skelmersdale in Lancashire and Cwmbran in South Wales. By 1971 32 new towns with a total population of more than 900,000 were being built, with plans for further developments. The cost of these developments comes from a fund which loans money to new town 'development corporations'. By 1970 of £1,100 million available £759 million had been spent. This money is being recovered from rents. By comparison with the crowded and unhealthy areas of many old cities the new towns offer modern housing, shops, schools, factories and clean air facilities. Recreational facilities are also being provided, such as the Billingham Forum in Co. Durham, but a frequent complaint is of the shortage of such amenities, particularly cinemas, and the distances to big shopping centres.

Despite the rapid growth of new towns most of Britain's population has had to be re-housed in the older centres of population. During the 1950's more than 3 million new houses were built and more than 3·6 million in the 1960's. Nevertheless as late as 1965 more than 3 million people still lived in slums, particularly in the largest cities such as Newcastle, Belfast, Liverpool and Glasgow. Those fortunate enough to secure new homes, tended to live even farther from the city centres unless rehoused in central tower block flats which have become a feature of most big cities. By the late 1960's it had been discovered that tower blocks had many drawbacks such as lift failures, noise, lack of playing space and a sense of isolation for the occupants. Most large cities—with the notable exception of London—stopped building these in favour of smaller units.

To reach these new outlying estates bus services have had to be lengthened and increased, whilst the inflexible tramcar and trolleybus services were steadily withdrawn. In 1949 there were more than 4,000 vehicles of each of the latter types in operation in Britain; by 1970 there were fewer than 100 of each.

Even buses have been unable to compete with private motor cars which swelled in numbers from 1·9 to 11·5 million between 1947 and 1970. Traffic congestion, notably at rush-hours, has steadily grown worse. Two major developments have taken place to try to deal with this. First there have been new rules about parking. Large areas of city centres forbid or severely limit parking both by time-limits and charges. Motorists have been offered multi-storey car parks and the use of disused railway land for long-stay parking. Secondly, many towns and cities have built by-passes, relief roads

A new town development

and urban motorways. Birmingham, Leeds and Glasgow have extended motorways deep into and around their centres. A more recent move has been the establishment of 'pedestrian precincts' in a bid to separate people and traffic. The new towns were pioneers of this but there appears to be a need for many more such areas.

New roads have been made possible through the rebuilding of old areas. New shops, particularly supermarkets and department stores, have also increased greatly in number since 1945. During the 1950's about 500 opened each year; at the same time more and more smaller shops disappeared. Cinemas and theatres have also disappeared from many towns, being converted into 'bingo' halls or warehouses. In a few cases two or three smaller cinemas have been rebuilt out of the former giant theatres. Many nineteenth-century churches and chapels built to serve the now decaying suburbs have also been demolished or converted to other uses. In the post-war estates the churches have been faced with new and heavy spending in order to reach the moving population. Admittedly, many recent churches are of unusual and striking design, outstanding among them being Liverpool's Catholic cathedral, and services have been 'modernised'; but even these changes have not stopped the long-term drift away from church-going.

The combination of an increasing population, earlier marriages and longer life expectancy has meant that despite the completion of more than six million houses between 1950 and 1970, a serious shortage has persisted. The greatest shortage has been where the best work prospects are, London, the South East and the West Midlands. By contrast, in parts of Northern England, Scotland and Wales it was possible to secure council housing immediately or buy at prices 50 or even 100 per cent below those of London. Purchasing one's own house has become increasingly popular. Most purchasers borrow from building societies. Total loans for this purpose increased from £733 million in 1947 to £6,037 million in 1967 and £8,751 million by 1970. Some of this increase was accounted for by price rises but by 1965 more than half the houses in Britain were privately owned.

Basically the problems of town life in the 1970's are the problems caused by a large and increasing population. The largest towns can offer the widest facilities, yet they frequently suffer from the greatest housing shortages, the longest traffic jams, the highest crime rates and the most serious pollution of air and water. There can be no simple answers to these complex problems.

Education

As the possibility of victory for the United Nations (as the Allies were called from 5th January 1942) grew stronger from 1943, the British government was able to spend more time thinking about post-war planning. In one field, education, it was felt that Britain had made little progress since the Acts of 1902. Elementary classes were overcrowded and ill-equipped. Secondary education was denied to thousands of children each year and higher education was available to only a very small percentage.

During the war a number of reports were produced, the most important of which in 1943 was called *Educational Reconstruction*. Most of the suggestions in this report were included in the 1944 Education Act. This Act related to England and Wales. Scotland's Act was passed in 1946 and Northern Ireland's in 1947. The 1944 Act set up the Ministry of Education to replace the old Board of Education. The Minister was to be responsible for operating a national system of education through local authorities. Local authorities were required to provide education over three ranges, primary (5–11 years) secondary (11–15 or up to 18) and part-time further education (15–18). The school-leaving age was to be raised to 15 and thereafter as soon as possible to 16.

Secondary education, it was decided, was to be offered in three different types of school. Grammar schools were to offer an 'academic' type of education to those thought capable of benefiting. Technical schools were to combine a general education with practical instruction (e.g. in engineering) and modern schools would provide a general education for children thought unlikely to go on to higher education. The problem was how to divide children into these different categories. An examination, soon to be popularly known as 'the eleven-plus' was established. But since there were few technical schools the energies of most primary school teachers, their older pupils and many of their parents revolved around the problem of how to secure the most grammar school places and avoid transfer to secondary modern schools. For it soon became clear that a place in a grammar school was an important symbol of success.

Criticism of this 'tri-partite' system continued to grow. It was alleged that the eleven-plus examination favoured certain children and could not with certainty select those who would do well at eighteen-plus; that there were proportionately more grammar school places in some areas than others. There was also the problem of the 'borderline' cases, children who had always worked well in class but had an 'off-day' or were unwell at the eleven-plus examination. It was not until the election of a Labour Government in 1964 with a promise to speed up comprehensive education that a real attack was made on the eleven-plus. Comprehensive schools, taking in all ranges of ability from 11–18 years had developed considerably from the early 1950's particularly in Glasgow, Leicestershire, London and Wales but were almost unknown in East Anglia. The supporters of comprehensives argued that not only was the 'unjust' eleven-plus done away with but large schools, with up to 2,000 pupils, could offer a greater range of courses and facilities. For example, languages such as Russian and Italian could be offered using 'language laboratories'. One large school could be provided with a swimming pool whereas four smaller ones could not have one each. However, in such establishments children and staff could easily feel 'lost', work could suffer and misbehaviour could increase. Many people were unhappy at the disappearance of long-established grammar schools which had been important centres of learning for the local community.

As a result of the policy of the Labour Government (1964–70) the number of comprehensive schools increased during these years from 189 to 1,335, overtaking the number of grammar schools (1,025) but remaining far behind that of secondary modern schools (2,690).

The reorganisation of secondary education as a result of the 1944 Act was followed in 1947 by the raising of the school-leaving age to 15. The decision to raise it to 16 was put off for many years (until 1972), mainly because of a shortage of teachers and school places. Many more children also stayed after 15, but these were mainly in London and the South East. Increasing numbers took the General Certificate of Education examination introduced in 1951 and during the 1960's the number of 'O' Level passes doubled. In 1966 a new examination, the Certificate of Secondary Education was introduced. Although the C.S.E. makes less demands upon sheer memory-testing it did extend the examination system to a further 20 per cent of 15–16-year-olds but by 1970 was still scarcely considered equal to 'O' Level. Scotland has different examinations.

The growth of secondary education since 1945 has naturally been very expensive. Until the late 1960's most expenditure went into the secondary sector but since 1966 governments have concentrated increasing efforts on replacing pre-1914 primary schools. Between 1945 and 1970 more than 12,000 new schools were built in Britain at a cost of £1,800 million, providing places for 6·4 million children. This meant that by 1970 two out of every three schoolchildren were working in post-war schools. This heavy spending on school building has been one part of a greatly increased educational programme. In 1951 total expenditure on education in the U.K. was less than £400 million or 6·8 per cent of Government spending. By 1970 this sum had risen to more than £2,300 million (11·9 per cent of total expenditure). Apart from buildings the major part of this spending has gone on teachers' salaries. Between 1951 and 1970 the total number of school teachers rose from 215,000 to more than 380,000. Most teachers in the United Kingdom have attended two- or three-year courses at one of almost 160 Colleges of Education; 25 per cent of men and 15 per cent of women teachers have attended universities. Increasing numbers of young teachers are being awarded the new degree of Bachelor of Education.

During the 1960's, higher education underwent considerable expansion. Colleges of Education not only extended their courses from two to three years (four years for the B.Ed. degree) but more than doubled their intake within five years. Universities have also begun to accommodate more students. Between 1951 and 1971 the total student population quadrupled and to cope with these numbers several totally new universities were built at Brighton, Norwich, Warwick, Lancaster, York, Coleraine, Stirling and other towns. By

1970 Britain possessed 44 universities and was bringing into operation the unique Open University. This offered part-time study for degrees to people who had had neither the opportunity nor the qualifications at the age of 18. By means of radio and television lessons, correspondence courses, evening classes and summer schools any enthusiastic and hardworking mature student can eventually graduate. In 1972 it was decided to allow 18-year-olds to attend Open University courses. The establishment of some 30 polytechnics has been another important development since the late 1960's. These institutions were formed from Colleges of Advanced Technology or Further Education and will ultimately have more than 2,000 students each. Polytechnics offer full-time 'sandwich' and evening classes to students who can obtain a variety of qualifications.

Most students, unless possessed of quite wealthy parents, are helped considerably through their studies by the award of a Government grant. This usually provides enough for living expenses and fees during term-time but many students do not receive full grants and so seek vacation jobs. Nevertheless, Britain is one of the very few countries in the world to provide this type of award to such a large percentage of her student population.

Law and Order

The increase in criminal offences which was noted with worry after the First World War has accelerated since 1945. The total number of offences known to the police in Britain rose from 720,000 in 1947 to almost 1·6 million in 1970. By far the greatest number of these in 1970 were minor traffic offences, such as unauthorised parking. With the rapid increase in car-ownership since 1945 this situation was only to be expected. Prosecutions for dangerous or careless driving, which help to produce more than 350,000 road casualties each year, have also increased. Since 1967 drivers suspected of being under the influence of alcohol can be stopped and made to take the 'breathalyser' test which measures the amount of alcohol in the blood. This probably did more than anything to cut casualties by 30,000 between 1966 and 1970. The use of the motor-car to help crime has also grown since the war, particularly since the new motorways now offer a quick escape route to or between large cities. The most notable example of this type of crime is the theft of wages being collected from banks. Security organisations have been established, equipped with helmeted guards in armoured cars, to prevent this type of crime. Banks have also been raided so frequently and their staffs threatened with shotguns, that larger branches, as well as those of the Post Office, have been equipped with heavy glass anti-bandit guards across their counters and with alarms directly connected to police stations.

The most sensational of post-war 'bank robberies' involved not an attack upon a building, but upon a diesel-hauled mail train of British Rail. On 8th August 1963 a well-prepared gang halted the Glasgow–London mail train which was carrying more than £2 million in old banknotes. This cargo was stolen after the train-driver had been struck on the head. An enormous police hunt led to the capture of most of the train robbers and prison sentences of up to 30 years were imposed. Little of the money was recovered despite the offer of large rewards. The continued spate of robberies since 1963 seems to show that determined criminals do not fear long prison sentences.

Bank robberies and other crimes of violence rose fivefold between 1947 and 1970. Since 1964 victims of violence receive Government compensation. Fortunately the murder rate has not shown such dramatic upward surges. The annual average through the post-war period has not exceeded 160 compared with 130 in the pre-war years. Individual cases, such as that of J. R. H. Christie who strangled six women and hid their bodies in his house in London, have aroused great curiosity and horror. Christie was executed in 1953, as were 122 other men and women during the 1950's. Undoubtedly, a large section of the public favoured the death penalty, particularly for murderers of children and policemen and those who used poison or killed several persons. There were, however, worrying aspects about hanging. Large numbers of convicted murderers were young, many under 20 and many had histories of mental illness or were found to have very low intelligence quotients. Derek Bentley, a 19-year-old Grade IV mental defective, was the outstanding example of convicted men of this type. Bentley and a 16-year-old companion who was carrying a gun attempted to break into a Croydon warehouse but were surprised by the police. Bentley was arrested but his companion was free for a further 15 minutes, by the end of which time he had shot and killed a policeman. At the subsequent trial Bentley was sentenced to be hanged, but the boy who did the killing was not. He was too young and eventually served ten years' imprisonment. Despite considerable public pressure Bentley was executed. Perhaps even more worrying was the possibility that a completely innocent man might be executed. Certainly, the subject of capital punishment, and to a lesser degree corporal punishment, occupied a regular place in newspaper columns, party conferences and Parliamentary debates. Between 1947 and 1965 the question of the death penalty came up frequently in Parliament and was abolished temporarily for a five-year period until 1970. Corporal punishment has also been abolished since 1948 except on the Isle of Man, where 'teenage' offenders are frequently birched. To cope with the rising crime rate the police forces of Britain have been increased, reorganised and re-equipped. The maximum number of police in Britain has risen from 63,000 in the late 1940's to over 100,000 by 1970 and spending on the police force has more than quadrupled to over £300 million. An increasing amount of this money has gone on communications and electronic equipment, such as panda cars, personal radios, teleprinters and computers which store criminal records. Another move to increase efficiency has been the amalgamation of forces. Small town forces have been merged with the neighbouring city or county police. By 1970 Britain had 67 separate police forces with an average establishment of 1,500 officers. Much the largest remained the 20,000 men of the London Metropolitan force working from its new headquarters at Tintagel House. Scotland Yard had become too old and too small by the 1960's.

To accommodate the prison population which had doubled from 20,000 (daily average) in 1947 to 40,000 by 1970, a considerable increase in spending has been made. By 1970 Britain's prisons were costing over £50 million per year compared with about £12 million in the late 1950's. Much of this, apart from recruiting new staff, has, particularly since 1962, been on new buildings and improving security. Nevertheless, serious overcrowding (three men to a cell) is still very common particularly in the older, nineteenth-century buildings such as Barlinnie near Glasgow, Wormwood Scrubs in London and Strangeways, Manchester. In a bid to reduce the prison population, imprisonment for the under-17s was abolished in 1963. In its place detention centres based on the idea of a short and very sharp shock for young offenders were set up. Inmates go through about three or four weeks of physical training, drill and 'fatigues', an experience so tough that few would wish to return. In 1967 the principle of 'suspended' prison sentences was set up for those first offenders not convicted of violence or other serious crimes. If convicted a second time the suspended sentence then has to be served in addition to any additional punishment.

The causes of criminal behaviour are certainly very complex and possibly different in each individual case. However, in one part of the United Kingdom—Northern Ireland—the massive increase in crime has clearly been a result of the violent political struggle there between the Unionists (who wish to stay with Britain) and the Republicans (who wish to join with Eire).

Between 1965 and 1970 (the 'troubles' started in 1968) the number of indictable offences known to the police there almost doubled from 12,846 to 24,810 incidents. Between 1968 and 1970 there was a 50 per cent increase, whilst during the five years above, spending on prisons doubled. Such was the breakdown of normal life and law enforcement that very few of the more serious criminal offenders were convicted.

The Nation's
Health

By 1945, as a result of wartime planning to meet emergencies, the problems of the nation's health were being tackled more fully and more systematically than they had been in 1939. Nevertheless, health insurance covered only half the population and even this did not provide either specialist treatment or hospital treatment. The hospital service itself was generally unsatisfactory with ill-equipped overcrowded buildings and long waiting lists for beds.

The Beveridge proposals (p. 178) for the establishment of a comprehensive National Health Service (N.H.S.) were enthusiastically taken up by the new Labour Government (July 1945). Aneurin Bevan was appointed Minister of Health and he set about his task with great energy. Even so it took three years of planning, committee meetings and Parliamentary debate before the National Health Service came into being in July 1948. Three major problems had to be settled: how to meet the costs, how to organise the services and how to secure the co-operation of the doctors, who disliked the thought of becoming 'civil servants'.

The problem of cost has long been the major problem of the N.H.S. It rose from £446 million in 1949 to 1950 to £2,175 million in 1970–1. Although some of this has been caused by rising prices, the service has at the same time been greatly expanded. About half the expenditure goes on hospitals and ten per cent each on the family doctor service, medicine and drugs and local health services (drainage etc.). Each worker pays for a weekly insurance stamp but this covers only a small fraction of the cost. The remainder comes from general taxation and, because the amount available is limited whereas demand for medical treatment is almost unlimited, priorities have to be worked out.

The administration of the N.H.S. fell into three sections: the family doctor service, numbering 23,000 practitioners by 1970, the hospital service which administers 2,800 hospitals through 19 regional groups and lastly the local authority services which are responsible for public health, food inspection and similar tasks.

The attitude of the medical profession proved to be the greatest obstacle to the establishment of a free and comprehensive N.H.S. Doctors feared that they would become 'salaried and badly paid civil servants under a National Board which would control all services, stifle incentive and research, interfere with the delicate and important doctor-patient relationship and even violate the secrecy of the consulting room'.[1] Bevan was eventually able to calm their fears and arrange a generally satisfactory method of paying doctors and also dentists.

From its beginnings the N.H.S. was very popular except, perhaps, with some who could afford to pay for private treatment and grumbled at high taxation. As increasing numbers queued for treatment, costs rose rapidly and in 1952 doctors received a £40 million pay rise. To reduce the cost to the Exchequer both Labour and Conservative governments (1951–64) introduced charges for prescriptions and appliances such as spectacles and dentures. The cost of the weekly stamp was also increased at intervals throughout the 1950's and 1960's. Nothing, it seemed, could prevent the remorseless rise in costs. Indeed with general inflation, and a deliberate policy of expansion of the N.H.S. through new hospital building and recruitment of medical and other staff, governments came to accept a constantly rising bill.

The establishment and expansion of the N.H.S. and the improvement brought about by advances in medicine has produced a much healthier population. Life expectancy (at birth) in England and Wales has risen for males from 48·1 years in 1901 to 58·4 in

[1] P. Gregg, *The Welfare State* (1967), p. 55.

1931 and 68·6 in 1970. For females the figures are 51·8, 62·5 and 74·9 years respectively. In Scotland and Northern Ireland life expectancy in 1970 was a year or two less.

The nineteenth-century epidemic diseases are virtually unknown in Britain today. The most serious complaints of the early twentieth century—tuberculosis, pneumonia and whooping cough—have also dropped in incidence. The number of tuberculosis cases fell from 85,000 in 1957 to fewer than 30,000 in 1967. These advances have been overwhelmingly the result of new forms of treatment, such as antibiotic drugs. Medical improvements have also reduced the amount of time which the average patient has to spend in hospital from 43 days in 1954 to 26 in 1970.

Two kinds of disease have replaced the older killers as the major cause of death in Britain and most of the industrialised world. These are heart disease and cancer. Heart disease, which is probably caused by a combination of factors, including over-eating of the wrong types of food and lack of exercise, was responsible for almost 250,000 deaths in Britain in 1970. Cancer accounted for more than 100,000 victims of whom one-third were affected in the lung and throat. Treatment of heart disease and cancer is continually improving but it does not appear that the figures *will* go down until people are prepared to change their way of life—for example, by giving up cigarette smoking. Road accidents kill almost 8,000 persons per year, although in fact, there was some reduction after the introduction in 1967 of the 'breathalyser' test designed to discover drivers who had been drinking an excess of alcohol. The numbers of those injured also went down in 1968 but the 1970 total of 363,000 was more than double the number treated in 1947 and naturally imposed a great strain on ambulance and hospital casualty services. With the vastly increased car population this rise might seem almost inevitable, but the separation of cars from pedestrians would do much to safeguard the latter. The compulsory use of seatbelts might also save many car drivers and passengers from serious injury or death.

If the 1967 'Breathalyser' Act reduced the workload on hospitals, the 'Abortion' Act of the same year increased it considerably. This Act which permits a woman, in certain circumstances, to have her pregnancy terminated, was passed in 1967 against considerable opposition from the churches and various charitable and welfare organisations.

By the early 1970's hospitals, clinics and private nursing

homes were carrying out more than 100,000 legal abortions annually. This was despite the widespread use of contraceptives which reduced the number of live births in Britain between 1964 and 1970. The percentage of births classified as illegitimate has risen steadily between 1957 and 1970. There have also been disturbing increases in venereal diseases since the mid-1950's, in drug addiction since 1960 and drunkenness, with a 50 per cent rise in convictions, between 1955–70. Although these are not at present massive health problems they have been seen rather as indications of a steady abandonment of accepted values. This has led to use of the rather doubtful expression 'the permissive society' to describe Britain in the late 1960's.

New developments in surgery, such as heart-transplants, tend to create the most interest and publicity, yet fewer than one patient in every five in British hospitals receive surgery. Of every five hospital beds three are occupied by the mentally ill and the aged, often sharing the same buildings. Working amongst these categories of patients is not popular amongst medical staff and because of the very large numbers involved they frequently receive inferior care in old and over-crowded buildings.

The success of medicine in prolonging life has thus created serious problems in caring for the aged. Only a small percentage require continuous hospital treatment and only a slightly larger percentage can be accommodated in residential homes, even if they are willing to enter them. Many hundreds of thousands of old people live alone, many of them in poor housing conditions and relying upon social workers and the W.R.V.S. for care and company. Some are able to live with their married sons and daughters but shortage of space and other difficulties often make this impossible.

Social Security

In his report—*Social Insurance and Allied Services* (1942)—Sir William Beveridge pointed out five major evils of society (p. 178) and proceeded to make suggestions for dealing with two of these: want and disease.

The setting-up of a comprehensive N.H.S. was probably the best means of tackling disease. Want or poverty can be created in many ways—by illness, unemployment, old-age and low wages having to be shared amongst large families. Beveridge proposed that a system of state allowances should be paid to persons in need which would always ensure that nobody should fall below minimum subsistence level. To remove any suggestion of 'state charity' these allowances would be available to all working citizens, in certain cases irrespective of income, who would all be required to pay for the weekly stamp. The principal systems of allowances were to be unemployment pay, pensions for widows, the elderly and the chronically sick and disabled, family allowances, maternity and funeral benefits and sick pay.

Both the major political parties promised to implement the Beveridge proposals. It fell to the incoming Labour government in

1945 to put them into operation. Labour had many far-reaching changes planned which were certain to involve Parliament in long hours of debate. In October 1945 it was announced that the payment of family allowances would begin in the following August. More than 2·3 million families began to draw 5s (25p)—for each child after the first—when the scheme came into operation. Total payments rose from £59 million in 1947 to only £174 million in 1968, for although the idea was to reduce child poverty increases have been given only at long intervals (the largest in 1968). Besides the obvious criticism that family allowances are spent not on the children but on beer or bingo, it is frequently suggested that they encourage large families at a time when Britain is very densely populated. It would not be easy to prove either of these allegations.

Almost simultaneously the Government introduced its Industrial Injuries Bill by which persons injured at work were to receive an extra high rate of benefit from the outset. If permanently injured a worker would receive a pension and so would his family. The Bill became law in July 1946.

The National Insurance Bill, the central piece of legislation, was passed with little opposition early in 1946. Each worker had part of the cost of a weekly stamp deducted from his wages and credited on a card. The remainder of the cost was paid by the employer. This stamp provided insurance cover for unemployment pay, sickness benefit, old age pensions and industrial injury. The 'insurance' aspect did not prove workable. More than half the cost of social security benefits has always had to come from direct taxation via the Treasury.

The new Ministry of 'National Insurance' (called 'Social Security' in 1966) was set up in Newcastle employing 40,000 civil servants. However, because 25 million wage earners and their dependants were involved, local offices also had to be established. These began work in time for the coming into force of the Act on 5th July 1948 the same day upon which the N.H.S. was established. Only on this day could the 1834 Poor Law be truly said to be dead and buried.

During the quarter-century since the establishment of the 'Welfare State' several important changes have been introduced. All administration is now in the hands of a 'super-ministry', The Department of Health and Social Security', which by 1970-1 had an annual budget of more than £6,000 million, compared with £2,500 million ten years previously. Britain also has reciprocal agreements with a large number of European states, the U.S.A., Canada, Australia and New Zealand by which the citizens of each state can receive certain benefits whilst in the other country. Completely free medical treatment is limited to a very few countries only, such as France, Sweden, Yugoslavia and others in Eastern Europe.

The first of the new benefits, family allowances, was, by 1970, being paid to more than four million families at a rate of £0·90 per week for two children and an extra £1 for each additional child. This was a very much lower rate than that existing in most European countries and has done little to reduce child poverty. The incoming Conservative government (1970) was known to be in favour of replacing family allowances by much larger benefits but only to families genuinely in serious need. One scheme, the Family Income Supplement, paid in addition to family allowances, had only limited success during its first year of operation.

The National Insurance Scheme was also amended, firstly in 1961 to provide for extra contributions and pensions for those earning higher wages and salaries. In 1966 this 'earnings-related' scheme was extended to provide a higher income for the first six months of sickness, unemployment or widowhood. In November 1970 the Conservative government began paying pensions to the small and rapidly declining numbers of old people who had already been over pension age in 1948. In April 1971 the qualifying age for widows' pensions was reduced from 50 to 40 and in December 1971 an attendance allowance of £4.80 was introduced for severely disabled persons over two years of age who need constant nursing attention.

The principal benefits, which still account for the largest percentage of expenditure, are paid in the event of unemployment, sickness, retirement, and maternity (for women who have paid sufficient contributions). In many cases, particularly amongst pensioners, these allowances are not sufficient to provide even the barest minimum living standards. To provide additional funds the Ministry of Social Security Act was passed in 1966 setting up a Supplementary Benefits Commission to replace the National Assistance Board of 1948. Anyone over sixteen years of age who is unemployed, but neither at school nor on strike, and who can prove need is entitled to supplementary benefit. The problem is to prove need and amongst several million applicants there are inevitably a few thousand fraudulent claims. The exposure of frauds in turn leads to calls for tighter controls of public money. The Department of

Health employs special investigators to check on possible frauds. Their activities, however, occasionally cause serious embarrassment to genuine claimants. This difficulty epitomises the basic problem of any social security programme which has troubled poor law officials and their successors since the sixteenth century—how to distinguish between the 'idle rogues' and the 'deserving poor'. The level of benefits must be sufficient to provide a civilised standard of life, but not so high that workers will voluntarily give up their jobs. Because some wage rates are lower than unemployment pay, it may be more profitable not to work.

However, with very large numbers of unemployed, old age pensioners and other categories of persons in need of help, the problem of the 'idle rogue' is relatively very small.

Leisure

Although British workers enjoy fewer and shorter holidays than their opposite numbers in the other major industrial nations, the amount of leisure time available is continually increasing. Most employees work an agreed 40 to 42 hours per week; the average man puts in five hours' overtime. Virtually every employee in Britain now gets two weeks' paid holiday, and more than half get three weeks per year, compared with only six days granted to about 80 per cent of workers in 1945. Since 1945 the five-day working week has become increasingly common, even amongst shopworkers, for a long time an over-worked group. Since average earnings have risen more rapidly than prices, the vast majority of Britons, excluding of course large groups such as the unemployed, pensioners and large families, are better able to enjoy leisure in the 1970's than their parents or grandparents were.

In the mid-1960's watching television was found to be the chief leisure activity of 23 per cent of the population. This was almost twice the figure for gardening, the second most popular activity. Older people spend more hours viewing than the 15–25 years age-group and more people watch in the winter than in the summer.

Television is essentially a post-war discovery. Although the B.B.C. ran a television service in the London area between 1936 and

A B.B.C. outside broadcast unit

1939 only a few thousand families owned sets. The service re-opened in June 1946, again transmitting only to London and the South East. However, with the opening of the Sutton Coldfield station at the end of 1949, complete with 230 metre high mast, most of the Midland counties and parts of the Northern counties were offered a service.

The B.B.C. made considerable efforts to increase coverage in time for the Queen's coronation in 1953 and it was estimated that 25 million people watched this day's events, compared with 12 million who listened on radio. By 1958 the whole of the United Kingdom could receive B.B.C. television.

By the mid-1950's, however, the B.B.C. had a rival in the shape of Independent Television. I.T.V. came into service in September 1955 despite enormous opposition from the press, the cinema industry, leading churchmen, the Labour party and other influential groups. I.T.V. was financed from the beginning by advertising and there was some fear that Britain might follow the American pattern by which the advertisers decide upon programme content. This did not happen and although it was a popular belief that I.T.V. programmes were less educational and more sensational than the B.B.C.'s the two networks tended to become increasingly similar. To offer an alternative, B.B.C. 2 programmes came on to the air in 1964.

The number of licensed television sets rose from 15,000 in 1947 to almost 7 million ten years later and almost 16 million by 1970. With the advent of colour programmes in 1967 the electrical industry has been kept busy and in 1970 nearly 500,000 colour sets were sold. Listening to radio has declined, particularly in the evenings, and the number of licences fell from 10·7 million in 1947 to less than a quarter of this by 1970.[1] The broadcasting of popular music attracts the largest audiences. Young people earning reason-able wages were able to buy cheap portable transistor radios which reached peak sales of 2·5 million in 1962. Despite the large amount of broadcast music the sales of records, particularly the '33' rose from 17 million in 1960 to 65 million in 1970. The sale of record-players has remained consistently around 500,000 per year.

Amongst young adults games and sports have maintained considerable popularity. Football, cricket, swimming and walking—6,000 people climbed Snowdon in one day in 1968—are the most popular recreations but in recent years more exclusive pursuits such

[1] Sound licences were abolished on 1st February 1971.

Holiday traffic on the Exeter by-pass

Holidaymakers at
Gatwick airport

as tennis, golf, sailing and ski-ing have attracted newcomers. By contrast, attendance at sporting events which reached extremely high levels between 1945 and 1955 has slumped dramatically. Association football enjoyed a revival as a result of the 1966 World Cup matches in England but many poorer clubs in the lower divisions have a struggle to survive. Rugby League and athletics depend heavily upon television fees and government aid.

Young people also make up the majority of cinema audiences, whose numbers have fallen heavily since 1945. Total admissions in 1950 were more than 1,396 million but by 1970 were down to only 193 million. As a result 3,055 out of 4,584 cinemas have closed during this twenty-year period. Television has received the major share of the blame for this development. Many closed cinemas have been adapted to cater for a new amusement—bingo—which is especially popular amongst women. Gambling has been made easier for men also by the Betting and Gaming Act of 1960 which permitted the opening of betting shops. By 1965 more than 15,000 had been opened. Football pools also continued to grow in popularity and during the 1971–2 season it became possible to win prizes of £400,000 or more.

Perhaps apart from television, the greatest changes in post-war leisure habits have been brought about by the motor car. By 1970 more than 11 million cars were on the roads of Britain by comparison with less than 2 million in the late 1940's. Weekend motoring has become very popular, creating long traffic jams between London and Brighton, Manchester and Blackpool and in the South West of England which now attracts more than 20 per cent of all British holidaymakers. The vast majority of Britons, numbering 34 million, still take their holidays within the United Kingdom. The relatively warm beaches in the south and the West Country and the mountains of Wales and Scotland attract the largest numbers. About 6 million Britons now go abroad, the most popular destination being Spain, offering sunshine and low prices. The Irish Republic which attracted one-quarter of all British holidaymakers until 1968 became less and less popular in the next few years as a result of the violence in the North. Within two years probably 500,000 British visitors were looking elsewhere. Italy has also lost some of its popularity with British holidaymakers who now favour Spain, but France has been gaining ground since 1968.

Acquaintance with the mainland of Europe may have helped to increase the popularity of wine-drinking in Britain. Between 1957 and 1970 imports of wine rose from 14 to 43 million gallons. In the same period spirits consumption rose from 13 to 20 million gallons and beer consumption from 25 to 34 million bulk barrels. To cater for this increased consumption the number of licensed premises in Britain, which fell dramatically between 1900 and 1939, has risen by more than 16,000 since the War to a total of almost 120,000. Figures for drunkenness convictions have also risen from about 50,000 in the early 1950's to more than 80,000 in the early 1970's.

   With opportunities for so many types of leisure activity it is unlikely that drinking will again become as great a problem as it was in the nineteenth century when so few other recreations were possible.

The Middle Classes

Since 1945 the increase in the percentage of 'white-collar' jobs amongst the total working population has continued. By 1951 almost 31 per cent of workers fell into this category. The number rose to 36 per cent in 1961 and to more than 40 per cent by 1971. The largest increase has been in the field of medicine—particularly nursing, science and engineering, accountancy and education—particularly amongst teachers and lecturers. The most notable declines have been in the Church and the armed forces. Clerical workers who constituted one per cent of the total labour force in 1900 now total 10 per cent and are mainly female.

'White collar' workers can, therefore, be found in a considerable variety of occupations. Earnings can range from considerably less than £1,000 per year for a nurse to more than £20,000 for a barrister or the chairman of a nationalised industry. The highest earnings are found in the 'professions' among people who have undergone long and specialised training, have a recognised qualification and who often work alone and unsupervised.

The most notable examples are doctors of medicine, lawyers and chartered engineers. Real earnings amongst most professions have risen steadily during the twentieth century but clergymen have suffered a 30 per cent loss and teachers and nurses have barely kept pace. To maintain their incomes some two million 'white collar' workers have joined unions, the most successful organisations being the older British Medical Association and the newer Association of Managerial, Technical and Scientific Staffs. Strikes amongst teachers became widespread in 1970. The National Union of Bank Employees on the other hand was for many years unrecognised by the large banks.

Most of the best opportunities for middle-class workers lie in London, the West Midlands, the South East of England and in Edinburgh. These are the areas in which are found Government departments, universities and research institutes and the new technological industries. Attempts have been made to disperse both government and industry but the effects have been small and London still acts as a magnet, attracting people from all parts of the United Kingdom. The continued drift of population to the South East since 1920 has meant a chronic shortage of housing and heavy pressure in these areas upon major services such as commuter railways, roads, hospitals and schools. The housing problem has been the most serious with a rapid rise in prices throughout the 1950's and 60's and an enormous rise after 1970. By 1972 the average price of a house in the London areas was more than £11,000, about double the price in many less favoured areas. For anyone moving into and exchanging houses in the South East the cost of housing became an increasingly worrying problem. To qualify for council housing very long periods of residence were normally required.

Many new and older housing estates, therefore, tended to be occupied by persons of similar occupation status and income. Frequently more than 80 per cent of the families came from outside the area. Moreover with prospects of promotion or better employment many middle-class workers stayed for only short periods of perhaps three or four years before moving on. Relatives were rarely found close by as in the older nineteenth-century types of estate close to the centre of big cities. Life in middle-class suburbs centred around the small family unit—and the television—and a wide circle of friends and acquaintances.

The children of the middle classes are bigger, stronger, fitter and far better at the basic skills by the age of seven years, a lead not easily reduced. They fill the public, grammar and top streams of

Expensive middle-class housing in South East England

comprehensive schools and are 25 times more likely to go to university than the sons and daughters of manual workers.

Apart from a minority of young people the middle classes overwhelmingly support the Conservative party. But it is thanks to the 30 per cent of the working class who also support the Conservatives that there have been in the twentieth century only three genuine alternative governments. These were the Liberal administration in 1906 and the Labour governments of 1945 and 1966. Members of Parliament, both Conservative and Labour, are overwhelmingly middle class in origin. Workers who get elected have frequently undergone a long 'white collar' apprenticeship as trade union officials. In the 1966 Parliament there were 156 Labour M.P.s who could have been described as 'professional workers' compared with 109 'workers'. The middle classes also tend to form a substantial majority amongst the membership of regional hospital boards, the Civic and National Trusts, parent-teacher associations and golf clubs.

It is sometimes said that Britain is becoming a 'classless' society. Heavy taxation and social welfare benefits have closed the gap between rich and poor. Certainly one cannot easily tell by outward appearances what job a man does or how much he earns. Thanks to higher earnings and hire-purchase facilities goods which were once only within the purchasing power of the wealthier groups are now available to all. Few homes are without a television, washing machine and refrigerator. Large and powerful second-hand cars can be purchased for little more than the cost of a new 'Mini'. Only the give-away final registration letter, introduced in 1964, indicates the age. Clothing prices have remained relatively steady, so that only the poorest groups in society face the embarrassment of unfashionable dress. Even foreign holidays are being enjoyed by young people whose parents could afford no more than a day-trip to the seaside.

It is the problem of housing that most easily segregates middle and working classes. Most houses are bought with a building society loan which in no circumstances may exceed the total of three years' earnings. For a man earning £40 per week, which is the national average, this represents about £6,250. If he has saved a further £1,250 the maximum price of a house he can afford is £7,500. In the South East and West Midlands of England in 1972 only a limited choice of smaller houses could be purchased for this figure. A successful professional man earning £5,000 per year could, by contrast, probably purchase a house in the £15,000 range.

Many manual workers, particularly in insecure jobs may hesitate about buying a house at all and would perhaps apply for council housing instead. In general, then, there is an overwhelming tendency for manual workers to live in council or cheaply rented accommodation, often surrounded by an industrial landscape and shortage of amenities, particularly new schools and hospitals. The less wealthy middle classes live in cheaper private property as owner-occupiers, and the wealthy and successful are again isolated in larger houses.

Until the widespread establishment of comprehensive schools there was also considerable segregation of children into the different types of schools. The children of manual workers made up the bulk of pupils in secondary modern schools. The sons and daughters of the wealthy make up the 5 per cent of children who attend fee-paying schools. Even the establishment of comprehensive schools has not helped to create a 'classless society'. Comprehensive schools in the large cities take their pupils from the surrounding neighbourhood, which may be a vast council estate or a large wealthy suburb, but only in smaller and more rural areas are they likely to contain a cross-section of social backgrounds.

In present conditions the desire for equality probably means a wish to be equal with those who possess *more* wealth and privileges. As yet the problem has not been adequately solved, even in the Communist countries which have undergone revolution in the name of equality.

Social Investigation

The numerous investigations carried out into social problems between the wars have multiplied on a far greater scale since 1945. There have been several reasons for this. First, despite the expansion and increase of Government departments since the early nineteenth century it was discovered, particularly during planning for the Second World War that many necessary statistics simply did not exist. Since 1945 the successive governments have set in motion many social and economic investigations, either by means of Royal Commissions, by grants to universities or other research institutes or by using the civil servants of particular departments. The results are usually published in *White Papers*. Secondly, there has been a rapid expansion of sociological studies in British universities and colleges since 1945. Major research projects have been carried out in addition to several hundred individual pieces of work by post-graduate students. Additionally, there has been a variety of investigations and publications by interested parties such as the Bow Group, The Fabian Society and 'Shelter' and also by The Society of Friends, and other religious bodies.

Government investigations, particularly those which have led to the setting up of Royal Commissions, have usually been concerned with very large and important social and economic problems. Sometimes the number of witnesses heard and papers submitted totals many hundreds. Amongst the more notable have been the Royal Commission on Capital Punishment which reported in 1953, on the Law relating to Mental Illness and Mental Deficiency (1957), on the Police (1962) and on Trade Unions (1967). Reports of Royal Commissions may expose many aspects of particular problems and they usually suggest remedies and changes. But there is no certainty that the Government will act on these recommendations, although some changes can normally be expected. If the suggested changes are thought to be too far in advance of public opinion the reforms may be shelved for several years. For example, the 1957 Wolfenden Report relating to homosexuality did not lead to legal reforms until ten years later.

One of the most important areas of investigation has, however, produced very rapid change in many ways. This was the area of the nation's education, where much of the progress described earlier in this section comes from a number of famous reports, such as the *Robbins Report*, dealing with higher education, the *Crowther Report*, dealing with secondary education, the *Plowden Report*, dealing with primary education and the *James Report*, dealing with teacher training.

Such reports are significant not only in respect of education, but also because they throw much light on society generally. In particular they have drawn attention to the importance of conditions in home and neighbourhood in determining just how good a person's 'chance in life' is likely to be. The evidence here has been supported by that provided by investigations sponsored by such agencies as the National Foundation for Educational Research and the Schools Council. One result of this has been the creation of 'Educational Priority Areas' in poor districts. In such areas increasing amounts of money have been spent to provide superior facilities in schools in poor areas and to attract teachers to work there. In this and other ways it is hoped to provide 'compensation' for children who come from poor home backgrounds.

Another important area of investigation has been into the continuing problem of poverty in our society. In this field individual workers such as Peter Townsend have played a notable role and to some extent research workers from the new universities have played their part. One of the problems here lies in defining exactly

The effects of the Clean Air Act upon Sheffield's environment

what is meant by the word 'poverty'. This is difficult because a 'poor' person today is likely to be well-off compared with a 'poor' person in Britain in 1870. However, definitions of poverty have been worked out, and investigations have drawn attention to a number of problems in modern society. In particular, the fact that many poor people simply do not know about the benefits which are available is, in itself, important. This has led to improved advertising of benefits. Another problem is that of the family whose head is at work but whose income is too low to keep them out of poverty. In such cases the family—at least in theory, but not in practice—would be better off if it was living on supplementary benefit and other allowances. To help such people a Family Income Supplement has been introduced. Once again the impact of social investigation is illustrated.

A third important area of investigation which has developed since the end of the Second World War is that of research into the environment. Increasingly it has come to be realised that industrial development, which admittedly can make nations rich and allow them to spend money to solve age-old problems, can also damage the future health and well-being of millions. There are, therefore, numerous investigations into this process, and one result has been the introduction of 'clean air zones' in British cities.

Other researches have included studies of the effects on children of being brought up in 'high rise' flats from which they can rarely go out to play and of the long-term effects of chemicals on human bodies. At present Americans have on average twice as much DDT, a much-used pest killer, in their bodies as Britons. The pollution of water supplies and the effects of fumes from cars are other areas that are being studied. All these, and similar, investigations are likely to lead to increased Government activity to protect the environment.

The Countryside

The expansion and modernisation of British agriculture during the Second World War produced a farming industry considerably more prosperous and efficient in 1945 than in any previous time. To avoid creating a post-war slump in farming as had happened in 1920, Parliament passed the Agriculture Act in 1947. This provided guaranteed minimum prices for most important products thereby ensuring a level of prosperity to the farmer and a continued supply of 'cheap food' to the population. In addition, the Treasury has been empowered to provide various other subsidies and grants to encourage hill-farming, the ploughing up of marginal lands and the use of machinery and fertilisers. Marketing boards, set up in the 1930's, have been encouraged to continue to control production, prices and sales of particular products.

As a result of heavy Government support which since the end of rationing has provided two-thirds of the farmers' net income, British agriculture has made large increases in productivity. This was despite the loss of 500,000 acres (202,345 hectares) of land for the building of housing, motorways, airports and factories. By 1954 agricultural production was 50 per cent above the 1938 level. By 1969 with 500,000 tractors at work and the liberal use of fertiliser, the cereal harvest was three times larger than in 1938. The development of scientific feeding enabled large increases to be made in the totals of livestock, while permanent grasslands have been reduced by one-third. The British sheep population remained almost unchanged between 1938 and 1969, but cattle, poultry and pigs have increased by 50, 66 and 75 per cent respectively. As a result, livestock products such as eggs and milk are produced in such large amounts that Britain is able to provide more than half the total value of her food needs, by comparison with one-third before the war.

Despite heavy Government subsidies totalling £382 million in 1950, but declining to about £300 million per year in the late 1960's, farming could scarcely be described as a popular occupation. Farm labourers' wages continued to lag far behind those of industrial workers as they had for more than 150 years. Hours worked are also longer—the average is 52 per week—and housing frequently remains 'tied' to the job. If the farm worker gives up his job he may have to surrender his cottage. Alternative housing is becoming increasingly expensive as many country cottages are being bought as 'weekend retreats' by prosperous town dwellers. Nevertheless the drift from the land to the towns which began 200 years ago continues. The number of workers in agriculture and horticulture fell from 900,000 in 1946 to 354,000 in 1970. This decrease has been made possible by the intensive use of machinery and through the extension of live-stock farming which requires fewer workers. Almost two out of every five British farms in 1970 had no paid workers at all; a further quarter had only one. Most British farmers therefore had to do most of their own work with help from their wives or perhaps one other man. Only one farm in ten employed five or more workers.

The average British farmer still has to work extremely hard. It is not uncommon to work eleven hours per day, six days a week. Dairy farmers work even longer hours than this. Farmers' wives also probably spend two and a half hours each day on strictly farm work. Although the farmer may spend an average of two hours a day on his tractor, he will still have a great deal of heavy lifting work and so is likely to suffer back and muscular strains. Farmers still learn 'on the job'. Most left school at 14 and only 1 in 25 have been to an agricultural college. Many farms in Southern England are run by managers employed by 'absentee' owners but although they are salaried employees, hours of work still tend to be extremely long by industrial standards.

Argyll Forest Park, 1966

A much smaller work force of 19,000 men is employed in the
countryside by the Forestry Commission which was established in
1919. During the First World War Britain cut down her forests
without any thought for the future. More than 450,000 acres
(182,110 hectares) were felled. As a result of the 1919 Forestry Act
more than 80 per cent of these areas were replanted by 1939. A
further Act was passed in 1945 with the aim of increasing Britain's
forests to 5 million acres (2,023,450 hectares) by the end of the
century. Financial assistance is also given to private land owners
who plant trees.

Most of the work of the Forestry Commission is concentrated
in the upland areas of Wales, Scotland and the Pennines where
conifers are planted. This is land unsuitable for agriculture. The cost
is quite high and there have been frequent arguments about both the
value and the appearance of these artificial forests. By 1970 the
Commission's estates totalled almost 3 million acres (1,214,070
hectares), of which slightly more than half were under trees in 380
separate forests. Sales of timber were almost 1·5 million tonnes,
much of it going not only to coal-mines but to the paper pulp
industry and to factories making wooden boarding. Many of these
factories have been set up close to the major forest areas and have
brought employment to Scotland and Wales.

The Forestry Commission's lands have also been used to
provide recreational facilities through the establishment of Forest
Parks. Four are in Scotland, one in Wales, one on the English-Welsh
border and one on the English-Scottish border. These total 500,000

The Countryside 229

acres (202,345 hectares) and are available for camping and other outdoor pursuits. There are also five Forest Parks in Northern Ireland.

More than six times the area of the Forest Parks is covered by Britain's National Parks. Each National Park has its own form of 'government' responsible to the Department of the Environment. There are considerable pressures from outside interests such as mineral exploration companies which threaten the natural beauties of these parks. Additionally, tight controls have to be kept over building, caravan parks and other developments.

Scotland has no National Parks but certain areas of outstanding beauty are under the strict control of the Secretary of State. In Northern Ireland seven areas were named in 1965 as future National Parks.

Considerably smaller in total area than the National Park are the 128 national nature reserves of Great Britain. Of these, one, the Cairngorms, takes up a quarter of the total area. These reserves are mainly the responsibility of the Nature Conservancy which receives help and advice from the independent voluntary organisation, the Council of Nature.

Historic buildings in urgent need of maintenance and repairs can receive Government grants. Between 1953 and 1970 more than £8 million was spent in this way on almost 1,700 buildings.

These attempts by both the Government and private bodies over the last 25 years to prevent further destruction of the countryside were certainly needed. They will be only moderately effective unless very large sums are set aside for river purification, landscape reclamation and other tasks. It is worth noting, however, that many lower-paid workers in certain areas may be prevented from securing a better standard of living if development permission is refused for, say, a new factory or airport.

Perhaps the most crucial problem which faces not only Britain but the rest of the industrialised world as it enters the last quarter of the twentieth century, is the effect of economic growth on the environment. More production will produce more jobs but also more pollution. The higher the standards of life the more waste is produced. But who is to decide when sufficiency is reached and a halt is to be called?

Possibly the deciding factor will be the eventual disappearance of the world's reserves of fossil fuels (oil and coal) and mineral ores (iron, zinc, copper, etc.)

Documents

The Industrial Worker, 1945-70

In the heart of present day British cities large numbers of people share few of the benefits which we associate with the affluent society. Living conditions such as described here have a serious effect upon the individuals concerned and also upon the life of the nation.
Shelter. Condemned: A Shelter Report on Housing and Poverty (*n.d. n.p.*), *pp. 44-5.*

Helen's husband is a coalman. They have six children.

'According to what they say we've got seven years left in these. We've been here eight years. They're just not fit to live in.

'When I came to it the bay window rained in at the front and the back kitchen wall was no good.

'The little back bedroom, I've never been able to use because it just pours down the wall.

'I've got four boys, and the eldest is nearly fourteen, and two girls.

'We've spent all we can on it. We can't do any more and that's it.

'According to them I need four bedrooms and there isn't any houses like that. So we've just got to wait until they get one.

'I just have to put the children in the one dry bedroom I've got. My husband and I sleep down here in the back room.'

She said that she was on the waiting list when they were married fifteen years ago. She would have been well-housed by now if she'd known that she had to re-register every year. She lost her priority.

'A man came here four or five years ago and said he was from the Housing, and could he look? I said, "What are you here for?" He said, "You're on the Transfer List." I thought that meant we'd get a new house, but I haven't heard anything since.'

Their children are: a boy of fourteen, a boy of eleven, a boy of ten, a girl of nine, a boy of six and a girl of three.

'There's no hot water here. There's nothing for the kids. I have to fill the tub up for them.

'It takes two hours to bath them. It takes you half an hour to boil all the water. I have to put two in and then empty it and then put another two in.

'When the big lad wants a bath we have to wait until the others have gone to bed, and then my husband goes out.

'When I have a bath they all have to go out. There's no privacy in these houses.

'My husband, he's the last for getting baths, 'cause being a coalman he has to do it every night, and he has to wait for the kids to go to bed.

'We couldn't have company in because he'd have to wait to bath until about twelve o'clock at night.

'For money I manage, just manage, and neither of us go out ever.

'He gets just £21 before stoppages, and he gets £2 of it and I get £15. We've had just one holiday since we were married. You can't save on £15 a week.

'We're not eligible for Supplementary Benefit. I don't get no free milk, and I get free school dinners for four of them. But the eldest boy won't stay at school for his dinner.

'About three months ago they put the rent of these places up. I used to pay £1 6s 8d. Now I pay nearly £1.50.

'Mind you if we moved we'd have to pay more than £5 a week. I couldn't afford that.

'It's just the sleeping and the hot water that you miss.'

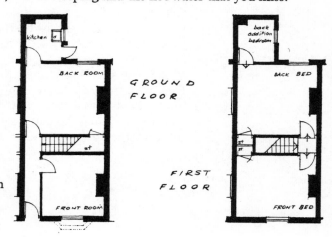

Surveyors Plan
Scale approx
$\frac{1}{16}$ to 1 foot

The surveyor reported:

'*First Floor*

Front Bedroom — Badly cracked ceiling—broken glazing—defective plaster—uneven boarding.

Back Bedroom — Damp around window—badly cracked ceiling—ill fitting doors.

Back Addition — Floor level approx. 1' 6" below remainder of first floor, no step down—sloping floor—badly cracked ceiling—dampness to walls—defective plastering—skirting board insecure. (Room not used).

Ground Floor

Hall and Staircase — No handrail to stairs—defective plaster—damp to party wall—ill fitting front door.

Front Room — Very damp to front and party wall—floor not level—door off hinges.

Back Room — Very damp walls—defective plaster—floor not level.

Kitchen — Ceiling badly cracked—very damp walls—defective plaster—cracked glazing—window unopenable—ill fitting door.

Externally

W.C. — Cracked pan, no seat—perished brickwork—uneven and cracked floor—roof leaking—rotten door frame—no catch to door.

Generally — Waste from sink cut short and discharges into back addition wall, instead of into gulley. Ground Floor timber suspended flooring will probably require substantial renewal, due to rot, evidenced by uneven flooring.'

Law and Order, 1945-70

The ex-Postmaster General gives his impressions of the Great Train Robbery.
R. *Bevins* The Greasy Pole (*London, 1963*), *pp. 121–6.*

In 1963 the House rose for the summer recess and on 2nd August I returned to Liverpool. There my wife had arranged a family re-union, and I hoped to do a little work without London distractions before going to France on holiday. It was not to be. On the morning of 8th August my secretary telephoned to tell me there had been a robbery from a Post Office train. He did not know the amount of the loss, but "it might come to seven figures". I said, "*Seven* figures?" and he said yes. I was soon on the London plane.

While I was Postmaster General I never had an uninterrupted holiday. No doubt fortuitously, crises always coincide with my absence. On this occasion my Director General was ill in hospital and his first deputy was off duty.

I shall avoid referring to any material which is already known from the newspapers: I shall reveal this unhappy story as I came to know it.

First, let me say the obvious—it should never have happened. The odds against it happening were at least a million to one. It is easy to say, as Graham Greene said, that it was beautifully planned. Whether this is true or not it could never have succeeded but for the slackness of British Railways and the ineptitude of certain Post Office officials. It was the combination of those factors that made the robbery possible.

First, British Railways. Every night a travelling Post Office, carrying mail and a crew of about fifty sorters, leaves Euston for Scotland. At about the same time a similar train leaves Glasgow for Euston. The train as a whole is protected. But special protection is given to the coach that carries high value packages, in specially protected vans. For this purpose there are three such vans—two in nightly use and one is held in reserve in case one becomes defective.

It may seem incredible, but between 2nd August and 8th August all three vans were either in railway workshops for repairs or *en route* for the train. This had never happened before. These are facts. For the first time ever their place had been taken by older and less secure vans. One specially protected coach had been taken off at Wigan on 22nd June with a "hot box": the second at Carlisle on 4th July with similar trouble: and the third at Euston on 2nd August with a buckled wheel. This was not surprising since it had been driven from Willesden to Euston with the handbrake fully on. Did the gang know this was the situation?

So on 2nd August all three were off the track. It was six days later that the gang struck. Coincidence? Luck? Inside information? Who knows?

Whose fault was this? Primarily British Railways'. These defects were comparatively minor and certainly should never have taken so long to repair—certainly not as long as one month or more. There was also, however, a failure in control by certain Post Office officials who knew the position but failed to refer it to senior officials who could have put pressure on British Railways to expedite the repairs. I at once took steps to make sure this could never occur again, but that should have been done by the administration long before and regularly checked. Even after the robbery had successfully taken place no one was admonished until I made a personal investigation.

So the mail train went ploughing through the night. In the second van there were five Post Office employees beside 128 bags containing currency notes worth £2,530,000.

Just after 3 a.m. the driver, seeing a red signal, brought the train to a halt at Cheddington. Three minutes' stop. In that time the engine and the first two vans were uncoupled. The van containing the loot moved off into the night for a mile or so and then stopped. The five Post Office men were then overpowered or threatened. The big haul began.

Meanwhile, what was happening in the rest of the train? It was carrying about fifty Post Office sorters. The answer is that, although the train was motionless for half an hour, nobody suspected anything was amiss. And this was true of the men who were travelling in the van immediately behind the high-value van—the van which, with the engine, did the disappearing trick. When the train stopped at Cheddington a senior official in the second van looked out and saw the signals at red. Soon afterwards two other men in the van also looked out. They saw two things. They saw the signal was at danger, and through the darkness they also saw two men standing by the couplings immediately in front of their van. They saw a third man join the other two. Then, through their corridor door which was open, they saw the engine and the van containing £2,530,000 move away, breaking the steam pipe as it did so.

One of the men then turned to his inspector in the same van and told him the front of the train had moved off. The inspector went to see for himself. He saw that the engine and the loot van had gone. He then walked towards the rear of the train to meet the guard. The guard confirmed the disappearance (it showed on an instrument in his van through the breaking of the steam pipe) and went to the rear to put down detonators. Meanwhile the inspector moved his staff forward in case of a collision from the rear.

Twenty minutes later the guard returned and went off in search of the engine. Twenty minutes after that the men from the raided van returned to what was left of the train and told their story. For something like three-quarters of an hour no one except those in the hands of the villains had any suspicion that the biggest robbery in history was in progress.

This is a story that begs countless questions. How did the gang know they were stopping the right train? How did they guard against a major train disaster in the night? On a line which is notorious for bad time-keeping they could not rely on the scheduled time table, nor, for that matter, on a message transmitted from a point say 50 miles away. Supposing, however, they had an accomplice ten miles up the line who telephoned to say "Here it comes—the next one, in five minutes." But if so, how did they communicate? By telephone? Which telephone?

How did they know the money was all in the second van? Observation in the early hours of the morning at Euston or elsewhere? Or inside knowledge? How did they know that on that particular morning the usual alarm system—which is both effective and frightening—would not be in operation?

How did they know that this one train would be speeding from Scotland to London with a consignment of unusually high value? That was not too difficult, for it is fairly easy to calculate that August Bank Holiday was 5th August: that people spend a lot on Bank Holidays: and that the banks would be ready to ship off by the Thursday train. I am willing to wager there will never again be a train robbery like that. I am not prepared to say why for reasons of security.

But there is one real lesson to be learned from the Great Train Robbery. It is not the physical precautions to be taken to safeguard money in transit or the technical questions of communication within trains or from trains to the outside world, although these are very important. But precautions can never be 100 per cent effective.

The fact that stands out is that such astronomical sums of money are in daily transit on our roads and railways that the wonder is that robberies are not more frequent and dramatic. Carryings from the Bank of England to its seven provincial branches are said to be staggering. The Post Office carries at least £4,000,000,000 a year. Carryings within London itself are fantastic, and so also are those between Companies and Banks and vice versa.

The second is that, despite representations by the Post Office both before and after the Mail Train Robbery the banking world was unwilling to deface notes intended for pulping at the Bank of England, so that they would be valueless to thieves and would no longer be negotiable in practice. Notwithstanding the events of August 1963 they remain unwilling.

Yet this massive ebb and flow of hard cash, with its great temptation to crime, will be reduced only when we abandon our reluctance to use credit instead of cash: when all wages and salaries are paid by credit transfer: when cheques are accepted by all and sundry, from all and sundry. Most of all, however, we need to provide credit facilities which most people can and will use. This need is certainly not being met by the Clearing Banks, with their restricted business hours. The banks really ought to wake up to the fact that credit is more civilised than cash—and can scarcely ever be stolen.

The Nation's Health, 1945–70

A Socialist view of the National Health Service.
Aneurin Bevan, In Place of Fear (*London*, *1952*), *pp. 75–7.*

. . . The collective principle asserts that the resources of medical skill and the apparatus of healing shall be placed at the disposal of the patient, without charge, when he or she needs them; that medical treatment and care should be a communal responsibility; that they should be made available to rich and poor alike in accordance with medical need and by no other criteria. It claims that financial anxiety in time of sickness is a serious hindrance to recovery, apart from its unnecessary cruelty. It insists that no society can legitimately call itself civilised if a sick person is denied medical aid because of lack of means.

Preventable pain is a blot on any society. Much sickness and often permanent disability arise from failure to take early action, and this in its turn is due to high costs and the fear of the effects of heavy bills on the family. The records show that it is the mother in the average family who suffers most from the absence of a free health service. In trying to balance her domestic budget she puts her own needs last.

Society becomes more wholesome, more serene, and spiritually healthier, if it knows that its citizens have at the back of their consciousness the knowledge that not only themselves, but all their fellows, have access, when ill, to the best that medical skill can provide. But private charity and endowment, although inescapably essential at one time, cannot meet the cost of all this. If the job is to be done, the State must accept financial responsibility.

When I was engaged in formulating the main principles of the British Health Service, I had to give careful study to various proposals for financing it, and as this aspect of the scheme is a matter of anxious discussion in many other parts of the world, it may be useful if I set down the main considerations that guided my choice. In the first place, what was to be its financial relationship with National Insurance; should the Health Service be on an insurance basis ? I decided against this. It had always seemed to me that a personal contributory basis was peculiarly inappropriate to a National

Health Service. There is, for example, the question of the qualifying period. That is to say, so many contributions for this benefit, and so many more for additional benefits, until enough contributions are eventually paid to qualify the contributor for the full range of benefits.

In the case of health treatment this would give rise to endless anomalies, quite apart from the administrative jungle which would be created. This is already the case in countries where people insure privately for operations as distinct from hospital or vice versa. Whatever may be said for it in private insurance, it would be out of place in a national scheme. Imagine a patient lying in hospital after an operation and ruefully reflecting that if the operation had been delayed another month he would have qualified for the operation benefit. Limited benefits for limited contributions ignore the over-riding consideration that the full range of health machinery must be there in any case, independent of the patient's right of free access to it.

Where a patient claimed he could not afford treatment, an investigation would have to be made into his means, with all the personal humiliation and vexation involved. This scarcely provides the relaxed mental condition needed for a quick and full recovery. Of course there is always the right to refuse treatment to a person who cannot afford it. You can always 'pass by on the other side'. That may be sound economics. It could not be worse morals.

Some American friends tried hard to persuade me that one way out of the alleged dilemma of providing free health treatment for people able to afford to pay for it, would be to fix an income limit below which treatment would be free whilst those above must pay. This makes the worst of all worlds. It still involves proof, with disadvantages I have already described. In addition it is exposed to lying and cheating and all sorts of insidious nepotism.

And these are the least of its shortcomings. The really objectionable feature is the creation of a two standard health service, one below and one above the salt. It is merely the old British Poor Law system over again. Even if the service given is the same in both categories there will always be the suspicion in the mind of the patient that it is not so, and this again is not a healthy mental state.

The essence of a satisfactory health service is that the rich and the poor are treated alike, that poverty is not a disability, and wealth is not advantaged.

Leisure, 1945-70

The Beatles. Early days and the way to success.
George Melly, Revolt into Style (*London, 1970*), *pp. 68-74.*

[In 1963] by the time 'Please, Please me' had got into the charts we knew a bit about the Beatles because the musical press had begun to make noises but, as far as I was concerned, they were just a new group, if a rather superior one.

Even so, when I was asked in the spring of that year to be one of the compères on the B.B.C. Jazz 'n' Pop Festival at the Albert Hall, I was pleased to see they were on the bill. (Incidentally, the title of the concert was, in itself, significant of the way things were going. For the previous two years it had been a straight jazz festival.) By now the Beatle legend was beginning to grow. There were references, usually patronizing, in the ordinary press. It was becoming clear they were something rather special.

I happened to arrive as they were rehearsing or, to be more accurate, fooling about. The producer, Terry Henebery, was *not* pleased. 'A couple of records in the charts,' he muttered to me, 'and they think they can do exactly what they like.' They seemed amiable enough, though, in the communal dressing-room.

There was a photograph of them in the programme, in neat suits and ties and what now looks like rather short hair. It was a very poor photograph in the show-biz tradition. They were all grinning and Ringo, who had by this time, and in the face of strong Liverpool feeling, replaced Pete Best, is showing some hairy leg between his trousers and Chelsea boot. I got them to sign it for my son.

What I hadn't been prepared for was their reception. It was my chore to announce them, and the moment I went on I was met by a solid wall of screams. In the end I just gestured into the stairwell, mouthed 'The Beatles' and walked off. The screams lasted right through their act. Beatlemania had arrived.

After the concert the fans gathered outside the stage-door yelling for George Harrison. 'We want George!' they shrieked. This was already an indication of something unique about the Beatles; the way that at one time or another all of them in turn have seemed to be singled out for popular favour. Theirs is the only group of which this has been true. In the Rolling Stones, for example, it's Mick Jagger and, less forcibly, Brian Jones,[1] who count but in the Beatles not only have they *all* their own devotees, but the emphasis has frequently shifted from one to another, and each of them has a separate function.

The replacement of Pete Best by Ringo is usually taken to have been on musical grounds alone, but I wonder. Ringo is not the world's most inventive drummer, but he *is* lovably plain, a bit 'thick' as a public persona, and decidedly ordinary in his tastes. He acts as a bridge, a reassuring proof that the Beatles bear some relation to normal people. The Beatles' intuition had told them that despite the angry crowds milling around outside the Cavern, they needed Ringo.

Throughout the rest of 1963 Beatlemania grew and grew. The papers fed it and it fed the papers. It wasn't, of course, the first post-war outbreak of mass hysteria, but it was on a completely different scale and on several levels. The teenage reaction was perhaps largely sexual, but the music, in itself, was fresh and interesting and very few people could remain indifferent or antagonistic. . . .

[By 1964] I was more and more convinced that Beatlemania was entering its final, if most hectic, phase.

There were several signs. For one thing, the hard-core pop fans were beginning to enthuse over Rhythm and Blues and in particular the Rolling Stones, a group who looked as non-compromising as the Beatles in their Hamburg days and gave no indication that they were prepared to shift an inch. Furthermore, the Beatles had begun to receive those accolades which, in the pop world, had usually turned out to be the kiss of death: the Royal Command Performance, the

[1] Written before his death in 1969.

flattery of politicians of both parties, the cooing approbation of elderly actresses.

Nor did their triumph in America—'Ringo for President' read the placards of the teeny-boppers—do anything to make me change my mind. Nor did their triumphant return; the whole of London Airport a-throb with pubescent enthusiasm. What had died was the feeling that the Beatles represented any longer a symbol of teenage revolt. I was certain that once their sexual charisma had burnt itself out, they would join, as the other talented products of pop had joined before them, the ranks of traditional show business.

What I hadn't allowed for was their own determination to do nothing of the sort. I should have taken the hint from an evening I spent in the company of John Lennon on the day his book *In His Own Write* was published. During the course of the party I suggested that despite his fame and money he was surely prepared to own up that not only did he owe a considerable debt to such Negro blues singers as Muddy Waters, but that objectively they were greater artists. He turned on me with sublime arrogance. He'd admit no such thing. Not only was he richer but better too. More original and better. We almost came to rather drunken blows.

Yet despite Lennon's confidence the early months of 1964 offered no convincing omens that the established pop pattern was about to break down. I'd heard of course that the Beatles were making a film but this was in itself no revolutionary departure. Steele too had made films and they had, if anything, accelerated his propulsion into the mum and kids belt. What I hadn't catered for was Alun Owen's script.

Until *A Hard Day's Night*, films about pop stars showed their early struggles, the big break and the happiness which success alone can bring. Owen's film did nothing of the sort. It showed the Beatles as the prisoners of their situation: on the run from fans, short of sleep and used by everybody. Instead of losing them ground it re-established their position. They were victims not victors. They were as trapped as any working-class boy or girl in a dead-end job. Despite being ousted from their position as the Number One Group in the *Melody Maker* poll by the Rolling Stones, the end of the year saw them back in power.

The première of *A Hard Day's Night* was held in

Liverpool. It looked as if nothing had changed that night. The Beatles appeared after the film on the balcony of the Town Hall. They were cheered by 50,000 people, but they didn't wait for the reception. They flew straight back to London.

Their doing so is a key to their long survival. They had, from the off, a formidable talent, perhaps genius; but very early on they recognized that in order to be free to exploit it, they would have to spend a great deal of their time in weaving and dodging. They knew that, in the pop world, the moment of total universal hysteria is the harbinger of complete rejection. Unwilling to accept the retreat into conventional show biz, the traditional get-out, they invented their own escape route.

Social Investigation, 1945–70

The last twenty years have seen a considerable number of coloured immigrants arrive in Britain. This extract describes the problems and bewilderment of an Indian immigrant arriving in Britain.
Ursula Sharma, Rampal and his Family (*London, 1971*), *pp. 73–7.*

When I arrived in the evening at London airport I looked around to see who had come to meet me. I saw all the people who had travelled on the same plane as myself collect their luggage one by one, go outside and drive off in taxis and cars. Everyone seemed to have some friend or relative to meet them. Surely some government official must appear at any moment and take me to wherever I was to be accommodated? You see, I was under the impression that if the government issued me a voucher, this meant that they would make all the arrangements for my work and accommodation, just as when I was a soldier the army made all the arrangements as to where we were to go and what we were to do. Surely, I thought, the government must need electrical workers or they would not have issued a voucher to me. Maybe they are laying electrical cables between England and France, or maybe they need men for maintenance work in their offices. Or else they will train us for whatever work they want us to do, like they did in the army. At all events, they are sure to send someone to meet us from the plane. I did not understand that the voucher was only a permit to work in England and did not assure me of anything more than the right to enter the country.

I kept on waiting and still no one called me. It was raining and quite dark outside although it was summer time, and I felt cold. I had left the heat of Delhi only that morning. 'What sort of place is this where I have landed myself now?' I thought. I looked about me and saw that there were only two other men left of my fellow passengers. They were apparently in the same plight as myself. We started to talk to each other. One had been a school-teacher in India and the other was a young lad of eighteen or so, but both had come like myself expecting to find work in England. None of us could speak much English and we were sitting there helplessly in what seemed like a kind of courtyard. Our luggage had been placed there for us to collect after the customs had inspected it and it seemed that we had been left there to die since it became clear that no one was going to turn up to meet us. Around us there was the usual bustle which goes on at an airport, people running to and fro, dancing about on their own business and taking no notice of us. So we began to discuss what we ought to do. Knowing no English, whom should we ask and how? We had not even any idea of the customs of the place, where we could go to buy a meal or how we could ask for accommodation for the night, nor could we see any Indian among the airport officials whom we could approach. We were in a tough spot, and all I could think was, 'Dear God, please get me out of this mess.'

Now none of us had more than three pounds in cash upon him so I said, 'Let us go through our pockets and see if one of us has some acquaintance's address. Then we can pool our money to pay for a taxi and all go there for to-night at least.' The school-master was the first to come across an address. He produced an old envelope which had contained a letter from a fellow villager now living in England. This friend had written his address on the back of his letter, but we were not even sure whether we would be able to pronounce it correctly to the taxi driver. The first taxi-driver we called could not understand our attempts to pronounce it at all and drove away unable to help us. The second one was not sure whether the name we were trying to say was the surname of the man we wanted to visit or the name of the road he lived in, but when we produced the envelope and showed it to him he managed to make out the address and told us that he would take us there. We stowed all our luggage in the taxi and sat down inside, feeling very relieved. The address we had given was in East London, but we did not know London and had no idea that it would be such a long way from the airport. It seemed that we had been in the taxi for at least an hour and we began to get worried. We asked each other what could be the matter. Where was the man taking us? Perhaps he intended to take us to some lonely place, then beat us up and rob us. After all, he was not to know that none of us had much money in his pocket. There would be no witness to the crime and as we did not know the language we could not even ask for help. But just as we were discussing what we ought to do in this dilemma, the taxi slowed down and stopped before a house. The school-master's friend ran out of the house and was obviously delighted at his arrival. He even paid the driver. He welcomed us in also. He sat us down and made us a cup of tea, and as I drank it I looked about me and thought how different this house was from those I had been used to in India. The chairs, beds, doors and windows were all of unfamiliar design and seemed very strange to me.

We stayed the night there and the next morning I began to consider where I should go next. Then I remembered that I had with me a letter, which I had received some time before my departure, from a fellow villager of mine who had been living in England for some time. He lived in Birmingham and he had written to me, 'Do not come to my home straight from the airport. It is a long way from London and if you get a taxi it will cost you a lot of money.' Of course I do not know much about the geography of England now, and I knew even less then, so had he not told me I should not have known that Birmingham was a long way from London. Anyway he had told me the address of an acquaintance of his in London and suggested that I look him up when I arrived. Had I not been so confused the previous night or had I not fallen in with my two companions, I expect it would have occurred to me to try to find this man in the first place. The address I had been given was also in East London so I explained to our host what I wanted to do and asked him if he would be so kind as to accompany me there, for I had no idea how to reach the place. He took me to the right address and left me with the man my friend in Birmingham had told me of. But this man turned out to be a real bastard. First of all he hardly gave me a gracious welcome. 'What have you come for?' he said. He did not even have the grace to say first, 'Come inside, sit down. We are pleased to see you.' No, all he said was, 'What have you come for? You can't stay here. Don't you know that I have only one room?' Well, I had not intended to bother him for accommodation, only to ask him for help in setting me on my feet, so I felt very hurt. Then he went on to say, 'What did you want to come to London for, anyway? I am a draughtsman and I have been out of work for eleven months, so what sort of job do you think you will be able to get, who are quite uneducated? Do you want to spend a year looking for work?' I replied, 'Well, I did not know anything about this when I came. I thought that the voucher ensured my employment. In any case our friend in Birmingham had told me that jobs were easily found. Perhaps you could take me to him and I could find a job in Birmingham.' 'That will be a waste of time,' he said. 'I was up in Birmingham myself only last week and I am sorry to say that our friend recently lost his job too. It is no use bothering him. If he can't keep the job he has had for six years, do you think you are likely to be able to find one?' This made me even more depressed because in India when a man is out of work it may be years before he can get a job again. That fellow so discouraged me that I felt as though my ship had truly sunk. I began to think that England was evidently not as I had thought it to be, not as it had been described to me. Why did no one tell me of all these problems, I thought? Surely those who had encouraged me to go should have warned me of these difficulties. How could I hope to get work if this was really the situation? Of course work is not really so hard to find, but I was not to know that when I had only just arrived. That man just wanted to discourage me and get rid of me as soon as he could.

DOCUMENT ACKNOWLEDGEMENTS

We should like to make grateful acknowledgement for allowing the use of copyright material to:

The Bodley Head for the extract from *The Deluge* by A. Marwick.

Mrs. W. H. B. Court and Cambridge University Press: *British Economic History, 1870–1914, Commentary and Documents* by W. H. B. Court.

The London Daily Mail.

Studio Vist Ltd.: *Britain between the Wars* by James Laver.

Lady Mellanby and the Cambridge University Press: *Recent Advances in Medical Science* (Cambridge 1939) by Sir Edward Mellanby.

William Heinemann Ltd.: *Angel Pavement* by J. B. Priestley.

Mrs. Sonia Brownell Orwell and Secker & Warburg: *The Lion and the Unicorn* and *The Road to Wigan Pier* by George Orwell.

Cassell & Co. Ltd.: *Into Battle* by Winston S. Churchill.

Shelter National Campaign for the Homeless: *Condemned: A Shelter Report on Housing and Poverty*.

Hodder & Stoughton Ltd.: *The Greasy Pole* by R. Bevins.

David Higham Associates Ltd.: *In Place of Fear* by Aneurin Bevan, published by William Heinemann Ltd.

Collins Publishers: *Rampal and his Family* by Ursula Sharma.

The extract from George Melly: *Revolt into Style* (London 1970) pp. 68-9. 72-3. Copyright © George Melly, 1970 is reprinted by permission of Penguin Books Ltd.

Index